Acknowledgments to Teachers

I express my thanks to the administrators of the elementary schools of Granite School District for their support and endorsement of this project. To the following teachers who enthusiastically welcomed expressive poetry and creative language experiences into their classrooms, I express my deepest gratitude and appreciation:

MRS. MARJOLET LEITER	Hill View Elementary	First Grade
MRS. MARY ANN JOHANSON	Upland Terrace Elementary	Second Grade
MRS. JEANNIE PENCE	Lincoln Elementary	Second Grade
MISS SHAUNA OLSEN	Carl Sandburg Elementary	Second Grade
MRS. EILEEN SMART	Academy Park Elementary	Third Grade
MRS. MARTHA MORTENSEN	Jackling Elementary	Third Grade
MR. BRENTON M. BAUER	Meadow Moor Elementary	Fourth Grade
MISS SHARALYN McKELL	Canyon Rim Elementary	Fourth Grade
MRS. MARIE MERRELL	James E. Moss Elementary	Fourth Grade
MISS RHONDA McQUARRIE	James E. Moss Elementary	Fourth Grade
MISS KATHLEEN LUND	Robert Frost Elementary	Fourth Grade
MISS DARI McQUARRIE	Eastwood Elementary	Fourth Grade
MISS JENNY HALL	Redwood Elementary	Fourth-Fifth Grade
MRS. MARIETTA KIRBY	Oquirrh Hills Elementary	Fourth-Fifth Grade
MR. TED A. PULOS	Crestview Elementary	Fifth Grade
MISS GEORGIA VEATER	Magna Elementary	Fifth Grade
MR. MELVIN D. GADD	Pioneer Elementary	Fifth Grade
MRS. SUSAN DOTY	Rolling Meadows Elementary	Fifth-Sixth Grade
MISS KAREN THATCHER	Rolling Meadows Elementary	Fifth-Sixth Grade
MRS. VEDA CHRISTENSEN	Roosevelt Elementary	Fifth-Sixth Grade
MRS. KAY TRUEBLOOD	David Gourley Elementary	Sixth Grade
MR. BEN F. BULLOUGH	Mill Creek Elementary	Sixth Grade
MISS JEANNE SNEDAKER	William Penn Elementary	Sixth Grade
MISS PHYLLIS BELL	Plymouth Elementary	Sixth Grade

Thanks also to the following additional teachers who contributed poetry manuscripts:

MRS. IRIS EPPERSON, Upland Terrace Elementary; MR. PAUL ROMNEY, Libbie Edward Elementary; MRS. AFTON SMITH, Taylorsville Elementary; MRS. CAROLE VANDEGRAAFF, East Mill Creek Elementary; MRS. JOAN BURRIS, Oakwood Elementary; MR. RICHARD WALKER, Woodstock Elementary; MRS. BEVERLY COOK, John C. Fremont; MR. MICHAEL RHEAD, Fortuna Elementary; and MRS. ENID BJARNSON, Woodstock Elementary.

Ona Patterson
Project Director

Foreword

Fragile as Butterflies -- what an appropriate title for a book that contains the inner thoughts and feelings of a child!

In our world of complexity, and oftentimes confrontation, how great the need for a quiet time for observation and contemplation. And greater still, is the need for expression -- in one's own way, and in one's own time.

The Poetry-in-the-Schools Project has provided this opportunity for many children; and in turn, their creations will provide enjoyment for children and adults alike, as these pages are read, now, and in the years to come.

Granite School District is appreciative of all the people who made the Poetry-in-the-Schools Project possible. Particularly are we grateful to those teachers who worked with children as they fashioned these delicate and tenuous thoughts of beauty for themselves and others.

Dr. Hilda B. Jones
Assistant Superintendent
Granite School District

Fragile As Butterflies

**AN ANTHOLOGY OF CHILDREN'S
THOUGHTS AND PLEASURES
IN POETRY**

Editor & Project Director
ONA PATTERSON
Illustrations by
Colleen Hinckley & Mary Gibson
Cover by
Tom Sjoerdsma

FRAGILE AS BUTTERFLIES

Poems wake up in the morning
  with a new idea.
Poems shine as the sun.
A poem is everything
  and everywhere --
Poems are fragile as butterflies!

ISBN No. 0-86653-116-5
Printing No. 987654321
Copyright © Good Apple, Inc., 1983

**GOOD APPLE, INC.
BOX 299
CARTHAGE, IL 62321-0299**

No part of this publication may be reproduced in any way without prior written permission from Good Apple, Inc.

All rights reserved. Printed in the United States of America at Whitehall Company, Wheeling, IL.

Acknowledgments

To the following professional poets, language arts consultants, and teachers, I express thanks and appreciation for inspiration and assistance throughout the project:

DR. MAX C. GOLIGHTLY
MRS. CAROLINE EYRING MINER
MRS. EMMA LOU THAYNE
DR. DAVID KRANES
MISS GERALDINE R. PRATT
MRS. MABEL JONES GABBOTT
DR. JEAN R. JENKINS
MRS. PANSYE POWELL
DR. ELLIOTT D. LANDAU
MRS. LILLY HAVEY

DR. FREDERICK S. BUCHANAN
MR. GLEN E. SACOS
DR. DARREL ALLINGTON
MRS. GAIL W. BELL
MRS. BETHANY CHAFFIN
MRS. GAYLE TAMPICO BOYD
MR. RICHARD A. WALKER
MRS. IRIS EPPERSON
MRS. BEVERLY COOK
MRS. MARIANNE PANNIER

Sincere appreciation is extended to the National Endowment for the Arts, Mr. Leonard Randolph, head of the Literary Program for the Endowment, and the U.S. Offices of Education for the Poetry-in-the-Schools special grant; to Dr. Walter D. Talbot, State Superintendent of Public Instruction; the Utah State Institute of Fine Arts; and to Granite School District for sponsoring this project. Special gratitude is extended to Mrs. Margaret S. Beecher, Utah State Institute of Fine Arts and to Dr. Ralf C. Riches, Assistant Superintendent of the West Valley Area for promoting and supporting this project in the Granite District Schools.

Dedication

To the children
Whose youthful wingbeats
echo poems for tomorrow's world
and whose "first flights" into poetry
made this volume possible.

Table of Contents

Introduction vi
A Poem Is... 1
Cathedral of the Animals 5
Color It Me! 15
Patches of White Clouds... 24
Haiku 25
Seasonal Corners 30
Once-A-Year Days 48
From Mt. Olympus 55
In My Crayon Box 57
City Scenes 62
Cross-Stitchery 64
This Is My Country 65
Hopscotch Math 67
Circus Sounds 69
Cats, Camels, and Caterpillars 71
Mother Ghost Rhymes 73
Lights in the Sky 75
Limericks and Other Green Things 78
Epitaphs 79
Silly Sounding Sentences 80
Poem Dust 81
From My Butterfly Net 90

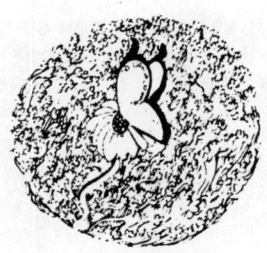

Introduction

FRAGILE AS BUTTERFLIES is a celebration of poetic sounds by young children that came about when teachers and poets introduced elementary children to poetry as part of the 1973-74 Poetry-in-the Schools Project.

The title for this volume is taken directly from the lines of an original poem written by nine-year-old Michelle Rosenoff, Woodstock School. This bit of metaphor exemplifies the delicate freshness and almost elusive quality of children's poetic perceptions and thought pictures.

Collected within these pages are children's responses to poetry, a new vehicle of language expression which mushroomed into the more than ten-thousand thoughts and poems during the school year. Not only was poetry a new experience for the children, but also for their teachers who attended weekly poetry workshops and took hundreds of ideas back to their classrooms. Although this volume reflects but a small portion of poems created during the project, individual classroom publications containing all of the poems written by each child were published by the teachers. These poems bear shouting testament of what can happen when children are provided with appropriate motivation and writing opportunity.

In this project children were given abundant opportunity for creative expression. Brainstorming techniques were used to broaden and extend vocabulary bases. Alliterative alphabets, simple similes, cinquains, haiku and free verse all became familiar classroom activities and experiences. Poetry was the seasoning that made language lessons, writing mechanics, vocabulary lists, spelling and reading assignments take on new zest and purpose. Poem consciousness, word artistry, and creative thought activities were woven into the total curricular scene as poetic composition expanded into all the content areas, including music and art. Caught within these pages are the echoes of delight that bubbled forth from productive classrooms as children gave bright ideas free flight, developed new kinships with words, and tasted the exhilaration and joy of creating something original and beautiful.

And then almost like an insect story, it happened! After the children had gorged themselves, like hungry caterpillars, with active verbs, descriptive adjectives, figurative language, and auditory poetic bombardments supplied by their teachers, a magical drama unfolded in the classroom. From gray newsprint chrysalises, wingtipped words like penciled silhouettes and rhythms emerged from the cocoons -- fragile as butterflies!

It is hoped that the reader of these pages can sense the fluttering of the youthful wings and experience again the myriad moods and tip-toe discoveries of a children's world that is but a few heartbeats removed from adult focus -- as fragile as butterflies!

Ona Patterson
Project Director

A Poem Is...

2

A poem is a silver ribbon
    Floating from heaven,
Don't let it fall —
    Touch the ground.
A poem is . . .

Kathy
Age 11

A poem is as long as a railroad track
Or as short as a pencil lead.
Sometimes it floats across paper
    like clouds float across sky.

Mike
Age 11

A poem is fragile
Like a bird singing
Watch a bird
And fly to different places
Like paradises in the sky,
And to far-off mystic lands
Where nobody has been,
    Just like a poem
        Just like a bird
            Just like me.

Chris
Age 9

As flowers blossom in spring
So does poetry bloom
    in any season

Mitzi
Age 11

Poetry is
a beautiful red-orange
and golden sunset,
filling the sky
with bright, blooming fire!

Lori
Age 11

3

A poem is wind
whispering by
Barely even touching you.

*Jennifer
Age 9*

4

A poem is a tornado
Powerful and strong
Like a sweeping broom.
It spins like a cobweb
Caught full of ideas.

    Shawn
    Age 9

The beauty of a poem —
A golden key,
  A silver chest,
    An opening to a path
Leading to the
  near future.

    Leslie
    Age 11

A poem
is a feeling
that comes
deep from
one's
heart!

    Heidi
    Age 11

Choose a subject to write on.
How about
  a cat, a dog
    a fish, a fawn.
Whatever you write
  It better be bright.
What can you see?
  What can you taste?
    What can you smell?
  Can you say
  Can you tell?
If this is the end,
  Well, well, well!

    Donna
    Age 11

Cathedral Of the Animals

The animals pray to God;
He asks them in.

Stacey
Age 7

PRAYER OF THE FROG

Dear Lord,
Help me to eat and swim well.
Keep me from the grubby hands
Who want to take me home.

    Amen

Adrain
Age 11

THE PRAYER OF THE TURKEY

Dear Lord,
Please hide me
from that monstrous mean human
who has nothing but Thanksgiving
   on his mind.
Please —
Give me the right colors to hide
and the speed to miss the blow
   of his ax.

    Amen

Miriam
Age 11

THE PRAYER OF THE ELEPHANT

Dear God,
Help me overcome this fear of little mice.
I'm so big and they're so small . . .

    Amen

Steve
Age 11

THE PRAYER OF THE ALLIGATOR

Dear Lord,
Please make me littler.
All the people in the zoo
Are afraid of me.

    Amen

Tina
Age 8

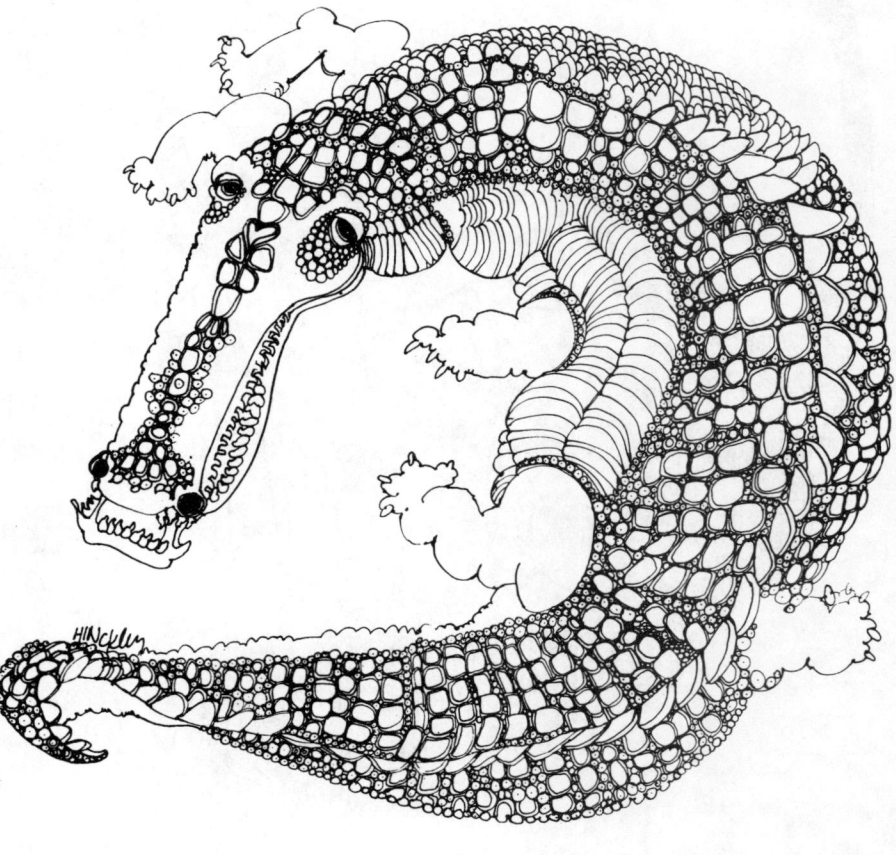

7

PRAYER OF THE LION

Thanks, dear Lord,
for making me king.
I am frightened
only by Man
who kills all things.

Amen

Lia
Age 9

PRAYER OF THE DOG

Dear God,
Make that dogpound so they won't get me.
Make me a license.

    Amen

Michael
Age 7

THE PRAYER OF THE SKUNK

Dear God,
My smell keeps enemies away
but nobody likes me.
Help me!

    Amen

J. Keith
Age 8

THE PRAYER OF THE LION

Dear God,
I ask Thee,
Why did you make me so mean-looking?
All the other animals fear me.
I sit all alone in the jungle
Like a king of the beasts.
Then why do I not have servants?
What of my crown, a wreath of hair?
My throne is but a mound
Of dandelions.
I sit each day
Just watching my kingdom.

    Amen

Michael
Age 11

THE PRAYER OF THE MUSK OX

Dear God,
Why did You have to make me
live in a place so cold
with so little food?
All the food I get
I have to dig for
    under the snow.
Why, Lord?

    Amen

Tom
Age 9

PRAYER OF THE PIG

Dear God,
I'm always so muddy
And I live in a dirty pen.
But when I am taken out of here —
    what then?
Will I be slaughtered and served on a dish
Because more people like me better than fish?
Oh, Lord, help me stay what I am
So I won't be made into ham!

    Amen

Heidi
Age 10

9

THE PRAYER OF THE BIRD

Dear God,
I am truly grateful
for the beautiful sky
You have provided.
Please save me
from that terrible fire stick
that kills my friends.

    Amen

Dean
Age 11

PRAYER OF THE ALLEY CAT

O God,
Why must I wander from house to house?
Why can't someone keep me?
Must I forever wander the wet alleys?
Doesn't anybody care?

    Amen

Tracy
Age 10

PRAYER OF THE ELEPHANT

Dear God,
I have such big ears that when
I eat my food my ears get in the way.
Please make them smaller.
I keep stepping on my nose.
I wish I didn't have such a long nose.

    Amen

Derek
Age 9

THE PRAYER OF THE ANT

O God,
Please keep me
Out of the reach
Of the terrible ardvarrk.
Please help people to watch
Where they step.
Encourage people
To have many picnics.
Oh, and one last thing, Lord,
Thanks for not sending
The exterminators
After me —
This time.

    Amen

Bart
Age 10

THE PRAYER OF THE EAGLE

Dear God,
Please help me escape
the punishing life I live,
for the killer, man, shoots
every chance he gets.
My nest upon a cliff is raided
by human kind,
    disposing of my young.
Rivers, streams polluted —
No fish for my young —
Oh, Lord,
Please help the human kind
    know peace.

    Amen

*Russell
Age 11*

THE PRAYER OF THE CAMEL

Dear Lord,
Thank you for my two humps,
They make me look so strong.
Save me from those pesty flies.
They bother me so.

    Amen

*Roxanne
Age 10*

PRAYER OF THE MUSKRAT

Dear Lord,
I am the muskrat;
I live in a hollow log.
Please keep the hunt men away
So I can make a nest for my babies.

    Amen

*Karen
Age 7*

THE RABBIT'S PRAYER

Oh Lord,
Save me
From the hawk so horrid,
From people
And from other animals.
Please help me
So I can run free
And eat
Without
Always watching!

    Amen

*Sherri
Age 10*

THE PRAYER OF THE DOLPHIN

Oh, Lord, bless me so I can be free
From the sharks that are my enemy.
And please give me strength of life,
And send me please, a dolphin wife.

    Amen

Evan
Age 9

THE PRAYER OF THE PANDA

Oh, Lord,
I am a panda.
I am so glad
I am black and white!

    Amen

Tyanne
Age 7

THE PRAYER OF THE DEER

O, God,
Help me keep from the dogs
    that chase me.
Help me that no more
    of my brothers will die.

    Amen

David
Age 10

THE PRAYER OF THE LIZARD

Oh God,
Make me fast
And give me big eyes
So I can see better.
Thank you.

    Amen

Kevin
Age 7

THE PRAYER OF THE ELEPHANT

Lord, thanks for this beautiful nose.
It helps me eat vigorously!

    Amen

Ken
Age 10

PRAYER OF THE ANT

Dear God,
Why do people always bother me?
If only I were bigger . . .
Dear God,
Please give me shelter
And some more legs
So I can run faster.
Thank you, God.

      Amen

*Dennis
Age 9*

THE PRAYER OF A TREE IN WINTER

Do not forget me, Lord,
I'm so very unnoticed
At this time of the year.
I've lost my lovely green dress,
And I'm so very frozen and cold.
Icicles hang from my strong limbs.
Oh, deliver me, Lord,
From this harsh part
Of the year.

      Amen

Jimmy

PRAYER OF THE HORSE

O God,
Why did I have to be a horse
And have people on my back so much?
Why couldn't I be like a rabbit
And have fun all day?

      Amen

*Astrid
Age 9*

PRAYER OF THE TABLE

Dear Lord,
They hit me,
Scratch me,
And write on me.
Lord, put a curse on the boy
Who sits here in fourth period.
Make him lose his penknife.

    Amen

    Jeff
    Age 10

THE PRAYER OF THE RABBIT

Dear God,
Every time I go out to get a drink
a fox or bobcat chases me.
I have a wife and bunnies to raise.
Please, God, make my feet run faster.

    Amen

    Mike
    Age 10

PRAYER OF THE SEAGULL

Dear Lord,
I live by the sea.
My sparkling gray wings flutter
When I have to do one sin —
   kill fish and insects.
Please,
Bring me something else.
I love thee.

    Amen

    Connie
    Age 9

PRAYER OF THE WOLF

Dear Lord,
Doesn't anyone like me?
Every time I am seen
I get shot at.
Why, Lord?

    Amen

    Vaughn
    Age 10

PRAYER OF THE RAT

Oh, thank you, Lord,
For making me so small.
I can do many things
That an elephant can't do.
(I like being little and gray.)

    Amen

    Patty
    Age 9

THE PRAYER OF THE PIG

Dear Lord,
Please give me better manners
So that other animals
Can stand to be around me.
I try, but I was created
   to be sloppy
And not neat like the lamb
   or the chicken.
Please . . . that's all I ask
   of Thee.

    Amen

    Sydney
    Age 11

PRAYER OF THE CHEETAH

Oh, Lord,
I can run very fast with the legs
You have given me,
but I have one problem —
Everyone wants to film me
and I'm camera shy.
Make them go away!

    Amen

    Andrew
    Age 9

THE PRAYER OF THE FROG

O God,
Why must I live
with this ugly green coat?
And I don't want to complain,
but this voice is bugging me.
I love this lily pond
and the green pad, but —
couldn't I have a beautiful brown coat,
and a voice like a nightingale,
just for once?

    Amen

Burton
Age 11

THE PRAYER OF THE DOG

Dear Lord,
Why make me chase and kill my cousins?
Why am I a prisoner of man?
They tie me up
   and pen me in.
Please, let me be free!

    Amen

Dale
Age 11

PRAYER OF THE MOUSE

O God,
Since I am the shortest animal of all —
I'd be much happier and taller
If I could just have a pair of high heels.
Although I'd look quite silly,
I'd be as tall as the cat
and he could not eat me.
Since I could not get in my hole,
I'd never get to sleep . . .
but I need something
so I will not be so short . . .

    Amen

Sidney
Age 9

PRAYER OF A FLOWER

Dear God,
Thank you for the love
I daily receive
For the kindness reflected
   on me.
I have grown
   and I have withered,
But Thou hast cared
And loved
And smiled.

    Amen

Kathleen
Age 10

THE PRAYER OF THE CATERPILLAR

Dear Lord,
Thank you for making me a caterpillar.
Crawling through the tall grass
   is such joy.
When little girls pick me up,
I crawl up their arms
   and have such fun.
But, Lord, I have a problem . . .
I have no desire
To become a butterfly.
I have one month more
In this glorious life,
And then — I must go
   through the change.
I dread it so.
Little boys catch butterflies
And tear off their wings.
Collectors kill
And preserve them.
Please, Lord,
Save me!

    Amen

Pam
Age 10

Color It Me!

MEMORIES

Memories of the past
When you knew me so well.
Memories of when I scattered pictures
   of me and you.

Lynnda
Age 9

SOFT SOUNDS

Soft is the sound of a petal
   falling from a flower.
Soft is the sound of a raindrop
   in a shower.
Soft is the sound of a kitten walking;
Soft is the sound of a lion stalking.
Soft is a cloud in the sky,
Soft as a feather floating by.
Soft as a pillow on a bed,
Soft as a prayer a little girl said.
Soft as a petal on a flower,
Soft as a drop from a May day shower.

Peggy
Age 10

Together
Is a wonderful place
   to be.
Only those who listen
   with hearts
     can understand.
Heaven is under our feet
   as well as over our heads.
So let it be.

Ronald
Age 11

BEAUTIFUL ME

Well, some are high
And some are low,
But beautiful me is in between.
And some have short hair,
But beautiful me has long, so there!
And some are nice
And some are mean,
But beautiful me is in between!

Brenda
Age 10

SOUNDS OF THE NIGHT

Through the night, covered with black,
Some eerie sounds come by:
The hoot of an owl,
The trees' rustling leaves,
Or a tomcat's mournful cry.
The color is pitch;
The time is ten.
I think these thoughts all over again
While I lie in bed and cover my head,
In fright of the sounds of the night.

Cathleen
Age 10

LONELINESS

All alone
No one
To hear of my fear.

Roxanne
Age 10

Loneliness is
   a broken bike,
    being fat,
     getting lost.

Mike
Age 11

Loneliness is grey;
It's dim and hollow
Like an empty room.

Kay
Age 11

Loneliness is the death
of your insides.

Terry
Age 11

After the sunset
I feel like
All my friends are
Gone forever.

Chris
Age 10

SOUNDS

The tiniest sound
is a church mouse
creeping quietly
across the padded floor
searching
for the last tiny crumb.

Greg
Age 11

Being alone is something special
I like to be alone because
My brothers wreck my thinking.

David
Age 10

SAD WORLD

No birds with wings,
No squirrels that hide,
No summer or spring,
No horses to ride.

No hawks with big, big wings,
No flowers that nature brings,
No woodpeckers pecking a tree —
Just imagine how sad
   the world would be!

Paul
Age 11

SADNESS

Sadness is the sound of a lonely sigh
As the rain taps gently
Against the window
And you have nothing to do
But wait.

Jenny
Age 11

If I could be the rain
I would splash down on the children
and make puddles
and PUDDLES!

Kelly
Age 8

QUIET

Quiet is silence,
And cotton, or pickles.
It's pillows and whispers
And a feather that tickles
The air that blows
Over fields of grass.
Although it's there
It's never seen,
It's quiet.

Janette
Age 10

Love feels like bells in your heart.

> *Kenneth*
> *Age 9*

My life has been a whirlwind of wishes forever blowing.

> *Mitzi*
> *Age 11*

There is nothing so strong
   as gentleness
And nothing so gentle
   as strength.

> *Steve*
> *Age 11*

WHAT COLOR IS LOVE?

What color is love, you ask?
Love is anything you want it to be.
Love can be friends.
The wind,
The stars,
The mountains.
Love can be any color or anything.
Love can be nature.
Love can be told in colors,
Words,
A smile,
Or a kiss.
What color is love, you ask?
Love can be any color you want it to be.

> *Ellen*
> *Age 10*

Love is a feeling deep inside
Love is a bad feeling
When someone dies.

> *Stacey*
> *Age 9*

Love is a thumb and blanket.

> *Michelle*
> *Age 7*

Magic
Isn't only
Pulling a rabbit
Out of an empty hat
Or making fire into candy.
What magic really is —
Is having love in the house.

> *Ted*
> *Age 9*

Be different.
Go your own way.
Do what you think is right.
Look back at yourself
   at the end of the day.
Do you like what you see?
What did you learn?
   What did you find?
Where did you make the mistake?

> *Stephanie*
> *Age 11*

20

Praying to
 God,
Starting with
 Dear,
Telling my heart —
Ending with love.

Janet
Age 10

Whenever I climb up the big oak tree
It's never crowded — there's only me.
I play on the branches up so high
And look down on the cars racing by.

Lisa
Age 10

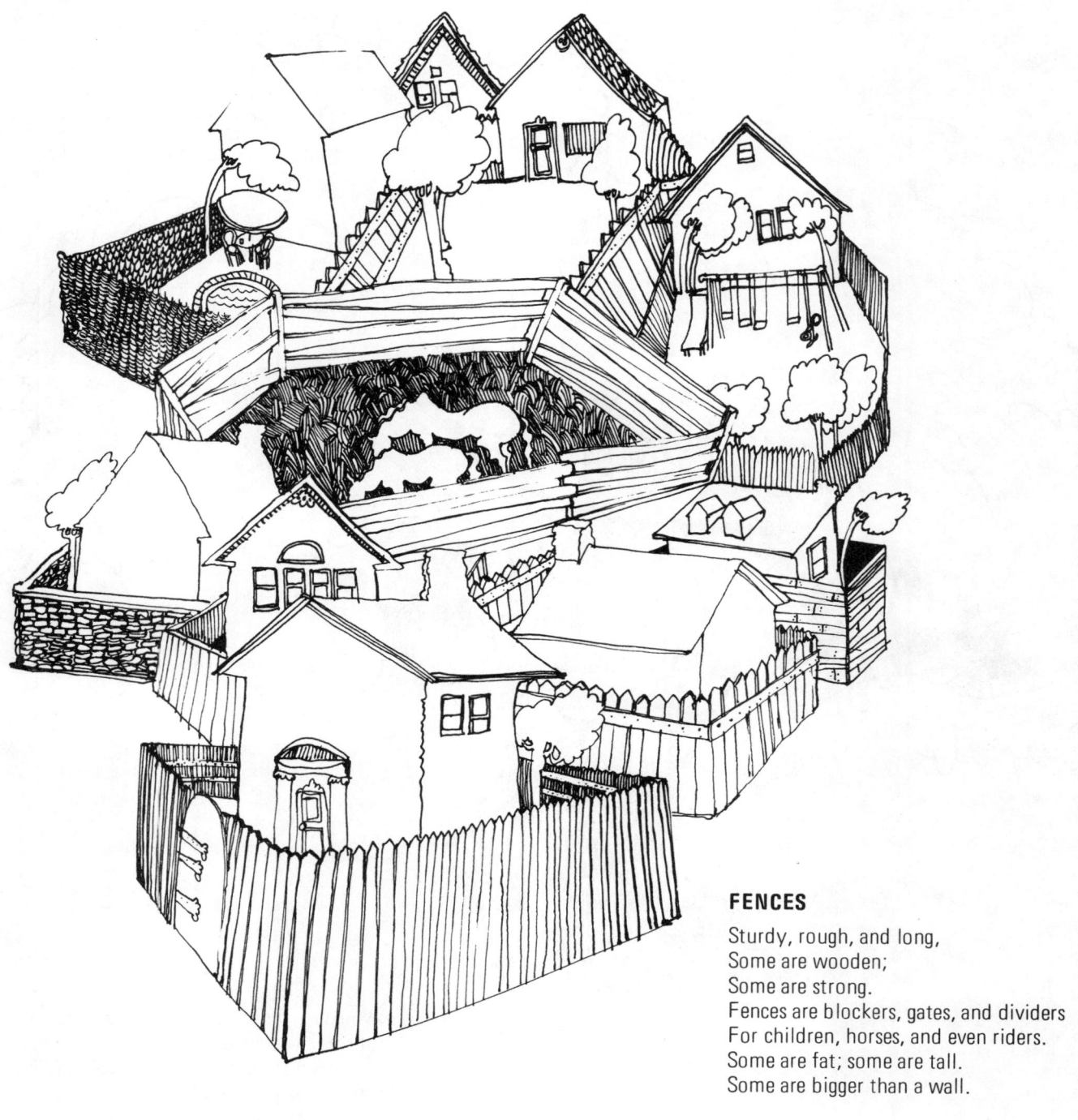

FENCES

Sturdy, rough, and long,
Some are wooden;
Some are strong.
Fences are blockers, gates, and dividers
For children, horses, and even riders.
Some are fat; some are tall.
Some are bigger than a wall.

Judy
Age 10

WHO AM I?

Who am I?
Why am I here?
Is life to love,
Or a thing to fear?

Why am I?
Why do I live?
Am I to take,
Or am I to give?

What use am I?
What can I do?
Were you my friend,
Or just someone I knew?

Is there love?
Is it great?
May I love,
Or must I wait?

What is love?
I really don't know.
Is it just there,
Or does it grow?

Who are my friends?
Who are my foes?
Can I trust anyone
Nobody knows?

Why am I happy?
Why do I cry?
Why am I living?
When will I die?

Andrea
Age 10

Is there space?
Is there room?
Is there something left for me?
Is there life?
Is there joy?
All these things I ask.
If there isn't,
What will be left of me?

Patti
Age 11

Patches Of White Clouds...

Patches of white clouds
    Like fluffy balls of cotton
        Floating in the sky.

Lynn
Age 10

I see my shadow
On the sidewalk in the sun.
It's so real, like me!

James
Age 10

The funny wet thing
    Dried its wings in the sun's warmth
        And flew far away.

Krista
Age 7

Green grass, tall and straight,
A hundred soldiers marching,
Waiting for the war!

Jon
Age 9

Haiku

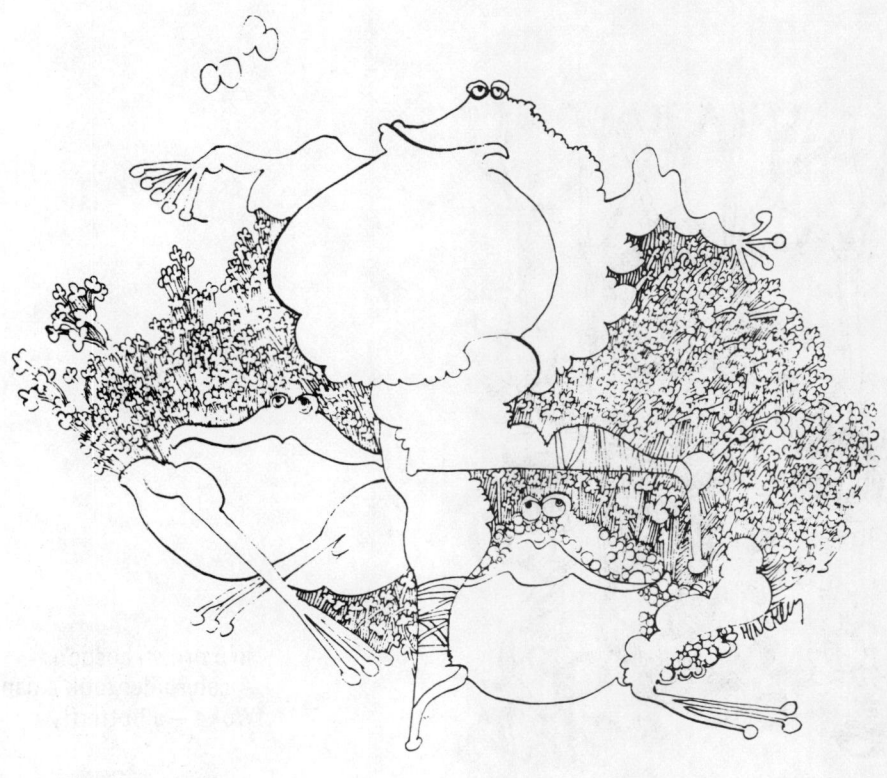

Tall jagged mountains
Scraping the heavens above.
Like knives held up high.

Paul
Age 10

Raindrops fall silently
Soft mist lifts from the ground,
The storm has begun.

Sally
Age 11

Slowly it opened.
It had become a butterfly
Lovely in the sun.

Leanne
Age 7

The cold, lonely trees
Stand up straight like brave soldiers —
Branches point like guns.

Gavin
Age 7

In a brown cocoon
A caterpillar took a nap,
Woke — a butterfly.

Shaun
Age 7

Patches of clover
   Stretch over the green hillsides
     In gay, cozy crowds!

Jeff
Age 10

MOUNTAINS
Mountains so far off
Rise majestic in the sky,
A symbol of peace.

Paul
Age 9

Like a butterfly
   Birds soar through the sky
     Wings fluttering high.

Debbie
Age 10

Engraved in red rock
   A waterfall is flowing,
      Rushing down wildly.

Susan
Age 10

Just like wild horses
Running down the mountainside,
The water rushes.

Lynnette
Age 10

THE FROG

A still green shadow
Sitting on a mossy leaf
Bumpy, spotted skin

Mary
Age 9

The funny, wet thing
Looked like a wet, shriveled leaf
Soon — a butterfly.

Christian
Age 7

Horses running free
Across the wild prairie flats
Racing with the wind.

Melody
Age 10

The green mossy pond
Like thick, colorful carpet
Feels cool to my feet.

Becky
Age 9

We watched the sun rise
Early on a spring morning,
Bringing life to all.

Greg
Age 11

One small white flower
Alone in a dark garden,
Waltzes with the wind.

*Tammy
Age 10*

PANSIES

Deep purple faces
Swaying, brightly dancing —
Soft ballerinas.

*Julie
Age 10*

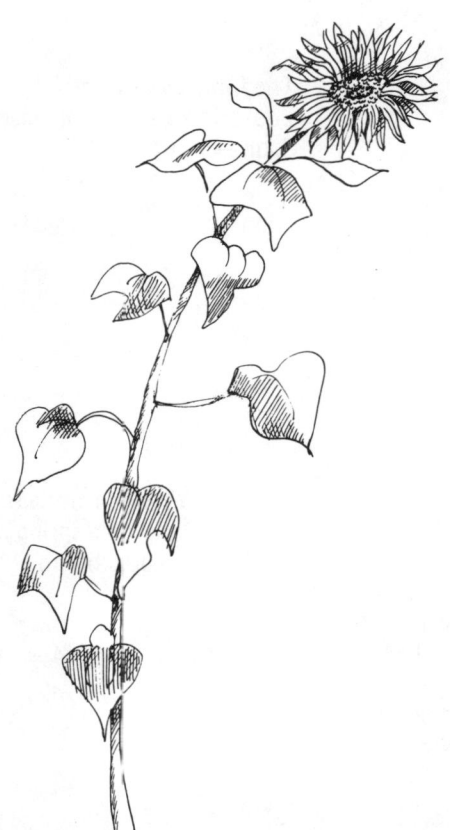

Beautiful flowers
Dance in their new green dresses
Waiting for summer.

*Christina
Age 10*

Soft, drifting white clouds
Lace the midnight sky with white.
The moon shines brightly.

*Billy
Age 10*

Free and gracefully
Bowing, just like a dancer —
The flower opens.

*Cindy
Age 10*

Floppy cactus spears
Shimmering in the sunlight
Like pine tree needles.

    Mary
    Age 9

On a sunny day
Pansy faces smile at me,
Waiting in the sun.

    Nancy
    Age 7

Neath indigo skies
And clouds of puffy whiteness,
A child thinks of life — death.

    Sally
    Age 9

LIGHTNING

A shining saber
Racing through the stormy sky.
A bolt of silver!

    Michael
    Age 10

In a brown cocoon
Lies a sleepy caterpillar.
It will live again.

    Keith
    Age 7

A FROG

Freckled emerald
Gleaming in the bright sunlight.
Splash! Water flies hence!

    Spencer
    Age 9

The great tiger creeps
Silently through the dark night.
Watch out and beware!

    Todd
    Age 9

Seasonal Corners

I walk through gullies
While colorful leaves float down.
Fall is silent joy!

Jayne
Age 11

Autumn is colorful
as butterfly wings,
Magnificent as a golden egg!

Cindy
Age 7

F ancy fall leaves are fun!
A ll around the town
L acy leaves look
L ovely in red, yellow,
     orange and brown.

Staci
Age 7

Looking out of my window
I see Mother Nature's world —
Mother Nature's truth.

Mark
Age 7

The whistling winds
   whirl
     and whiz
       past my windows
         waiting for winter.

Kenny
Age 7

OCTOBER
In Grandpa's corn patch
October wind is blowing.
Fall is here for good.

Mitzi
Age 11

MIDDLE OF OCTOBER

In a pumpkin patch
A pumpkin sits quietly
On a frosty night
Waiting.

Sally
Age 11

AUTUMN

The mountains
are a
patchwork quilt.

Paul
Age 11

Like wind brushing clouds,
Jack Frost is painting his last
Until next winter.

Brian
Age 10

FALL

Silver branches,
Shiny coins,
I collect coins from the ground —
A basket of shiny, sparkly,
Golden coins.

Jimmy
Age 10

Autumn is here
Rumpled yellow paint
Covers the ground —
Tracked up to the door.

Pam
Age 11

Autumn leaves
Crunchy
Ugly
Dried-up leaves
Waiting to be jumped in.

Ned
Age 7

Caterpillars are awakening —
Realizing they are butterflies.

Carol
Age 10

Fall is oak leaves
brown
squiggly and crackly.

Troy
Age 6

AUTUMN

Dry crackling leaves
Hanging on for dear life!

Brenda
Age 11

The tangled, twisted trees
knew the cold was near.
They showed-off
in their new coats.

Scott
Age 11

WHY DOES AUTUMN HAVE TO GO?

The moon is high in the autumn sky
The air is damp and cool,
I sigh and wonder why I have to go to school.
I love the crackly autumn leaves
    rustling in the breeze,
The autumn sun in the autumn sky
    is so wonderful to see.
I look at the pretty autumn leaves
    falling down so slow,
Then I wonder with a sigh —
Why does autumn have to go?

Ewen
Age 9

The colorful mountains are when Mother Nature spills her paint.

Kellie
Age 10

The aged oaks are Paul Bunyan's toothpicks.

Paige
Age 10

The trees are long, thin monsters
Growing out of the ground
With arms to grab the air.

Sheri
Age 9

Leaves off a tree fall
Very lightly and softly
Like petals in spring.

Tammy
Age 10

Feathers fall on my windows.
Are the angels pillow fighting?

> Glenn
> Age 11

Crystal jewels look like sparkling stars
   dazzling in the sky.
The bubbly clouds look like
   a cottony pincushion.
Icy wind rattles at the windowpane.

> Leslie
> Age 11

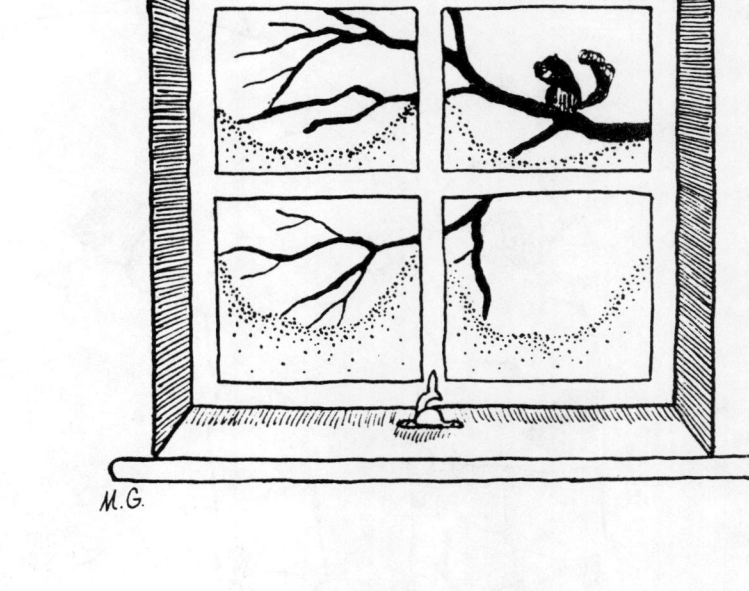

Cold and very sad
The winter trees stand lonely —
Waiting for the sun.

> Merridee
> Age 7

My tree is lonely —
He needs a leaf on his branch.
Bitter wind, in the sky
Stop blowing!

> Lisa
> Age 7

WAITING FOR WINTER

Waiting and waiting
The wind whispers across my window,
Wishing that snow would fall.
Why is the wind
Walking across the sky,
Whining and whispering to himself?
When is winter going to come?
While waiting
The wind sees a little white thing fall,
Then he whispers to himself,
Winter has come after all.

> Cindy
> Age 7

The trees are bare now,
Winter is stretching down.
The bitter stillness begins.

> Renee
> Age 10

Falling frost
Softly drifting
To make the crystal blankets bigger,
Leaving the little flakes
Cornered by the windows
behind
forever.

> Lori
> Age 11

SNOW

A snow blanket
Pretty, white —
A cotton ball
Puffy, light —
From the sky,
Like bits —
Like diamond rings
Still fall.

Valerie
Age 7

The bite of winter
  stings your nose and toes cold
And never lets go.

Wendy
Age 9

Snow is falling on the ground.
Are clouds coming apart?

Apryl
Age 10

TO FROSTY

Oh, little white man
With your big black eyes,
And your orange nose,
And your cut-charcoal smile,
Why do you stand
So still?

Gary
Age 10

SNOW

Snow is like ice cream
And marshmallows
And vanilla.
Snow can be creamy white
And crunchy
And melty —
Like a white rabbit or two,
Or tile in a tub,
Or chalk on a smooth piece of paper.

Michael
Age 6

JANUARY SCENE

Trees are ivory arches.
The rabbit tracks silent.
The swish of a hockey puck slides along.
Your breath is foggy breeze . . .
In January.

Kirk
Age 11

WINTER WIND

Whispering, white wind.
Wishing, wishing for snow.
Walk through the wild, wintery snow.

Tricia
Age 7

Night flows on —
An ivory sheet of snow
    is being laid.
A misty cloud looks on.

Glenn
Age 11

FOG

When fog comes
The sun looks like a ball
Hanging in the sky.
Fog is a magician
Making things disappear
With his magic wand.

Mark
Age 7

Snow
Looks beautiful
As it shivers down
Through the bitter sky.

Shelly
Age 9

WINTER

Wild wintery winds blow
    Over cold, tall forest trees.
        An icy gray sky
            Looks down at the cold ground --
Cold, mean, bleak Winter!

Mark
Age 7

Miss Winter's coat is made of fine white fur,
But when she gets angry
She throws it in a fit,
And all the world blurs white.

Mitzi
Age 11

SNOWMAN

Lifeless balls of snow,
A carrot nose and buttons
Are melting away.

Carol
Age 9

Silence all around,
Softly, gently, quietly
A snowflake falls.

*Barbara
Age 11*

Snow
Has a fluffy way of falling.
It falls as if it were
a bunch of feathers.
The snow is so thin,
It is just like
A sift of wind.

*Robb
Age 10*

Skating.
Slipping.
Falling.
Sliding all over the wet ice.
Getting bruised all over,
That hurts!

*Peggy
Age 10*

The winter snow blows so fast,
It bites noses,
And tickles toeses,
And gives me coldses.

*Shawn
Age 11*

Snow-capped mountains;
Icing on a cake.

Bob

I like snow
Because my sister and I
Open up our mouths
And the snow goes in!

*Tricia
Age 7*

Snow nuzzles
   down
      to the ground.

*Eric
Age 6*

Winter makes me think of marshmallows,
Yummy and chewy,
Vanilla ice cream, cold and white,
Clouds that are fluffy,
And just seem to glide away.
But what I have to do . . .
   is SHOVEL!

*Kevin
Age 6*

Fog lights gracefully on the world
Like a chorus of dove feathers
Falling.

*Todd
Age 11*

Our sleds lick the ice!

*Debbie
Age 9*

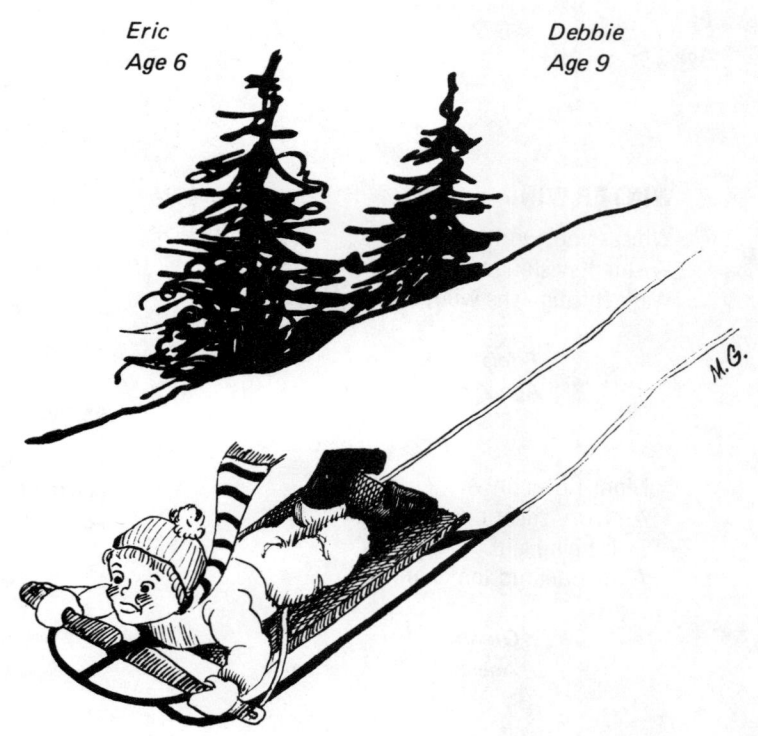

The heavy, white snow
   settles upon the pine boughs
      like gigantic claws.

Laura
Age 10

SNOWFLAKES

Snowflakes are
      feathers
    falling from the moon,
  glittering jewels and diamonds.
Snowflakes are
      breadcrumbs
    falling to the ground
  for the snowbirds to eat.

Mark
Age 7

Winter trees,
All bald,
They wait and wait
For summer.
At night
They look like ghosts
Shining in the night.

Carey
Age 7

WINTER TREES

Every winter night
  the witches
    come out,
And change trees
  into spiders
    and spider webs,
So they can catch people
  in the darkness
    of the night.

Tammy
Age 7

WHAT IS A SNOWFLAKE?

It looks like
A quivering bird
With wings
Like sparkly, crystal stars.
It is a ghostly fairy tale.

Valerie
Age 7

Snow flowers
Blooming
With lonely delight.

Janet
Age 11

FROST-DAISIES

On the meadow
I see a silver blanket
Where there once was one of green.
And I hear the brittle ice
Crackling as I walk,
While dazzling frost-daisies
Dance in the crystal skies.

Teresa
Age 11

Snow is a big fluffy coat on the ground.

Stephen
Age 7

I feel the sweet glow of spring coming back
And winter is marching out!

Tim
Age 9

Bare trees
are waiting
for spring to come
and bring back their leaves.

Rick
Age 7

Spring is a corner
between winter and summer!

Greg
Age 11

March is the time when spring awakens
and ponds and lakes
smile at you.

Lena
Age 10

WINTER TREES

The trees are bald in winter
With spooky hands.
The trees
Are big spiders
Fighting with dragons.

Troy
Age 7

WINTER

On a gloomy day
The smell of spring
  is far away.
The trees are bare.
The mountains are hiding.
I have an unhappy feeling inside.

Miranda
Age 6

TREES IN WINTER

Tall, bare, branchy wintry trees,
Waiting for leaves to grow.
Frosty, empty, birds' nests
Waiting for birds to move in.
Frosty, sad trees —
But with the promise of life
Once again
In spring.

Jay
Age 7

Wind is like the breath of a giant god
Blowing forevers
Into the sky.

Scott
Age 9

Thunder is the North and South Winds arguing together,
Slashing each other with lightning whips
And bleeding rain upon us.

Michael
Age 9

Lightning is a jagged knife
Being thrown by the North Wind
In the sky

Lyndon
Age 9

March is when nature
   sleepily awakens
      to show us beauty.

Sharon
Age 9

Branches bowed
  Swayed and danced
In the howling
  Roaring
    Pounding
      Snapping
        Whistling
          Thundering
            Hammering
              Wind.

Tracy
Age 9

WIND
Wind blows
Wind whines
Sometimes it hits you
From behind.

Steve
Age 11

It's a day of pussy willows,
They're swaying from head to head.
It looks like a battle
   between the willows and the wind!

June
Age 11

Spring is when bikes and kites are king!

Steffanie
Age 7

I wish
the wind would whisper
in the woods
when I take a walk!

Kevin
Age 7

MY KITE

It grows up so far in the air
And blooms
In the sky.

Danny
Age 7

M ysterious wind
A n air of excitement
R acing through the clouds
C harged atmosphere
H owling, hungry monster!

Jacque
Age 7

The wind is a giant
blowing his breath
through the little town.
Howling, sighing, blowing.

Robyn
Age 9

K inks in the string
I nching upward
T angled again
E rratic flyer

Kenny
Age 10

The wind blows
and whistles
and twirls
with little scary movements.
It's cold
and chasing you.
Watch out!

Roberta
Age 9

MARCH

In like a lion —
Musty dirt in our eyes,
Spring is on its way.
Gushing winds come in March.
Cans fly into the fences.
Horrible winds take things
In March!

Mark
Age 7

WIND

The wind is very anonymous.
All night it howls like a wolf
And makes trees fall down
And the grasses blow.
But when you listen,
It dies down.
And when you go out to catch it —
All you get is cold.

Danny
Age 9

Spring is a windy bottle of scents!

*Brook
Age 11*

The kite can't play
without any wind!

*Alexia
Age 6*

WIND

March monster walking in
With big arms pushing us away
And now he wants to fly my kite!

*Darin
Age 10*

WIND

The wind
is a strong waterfall
rushing
to break the dam.

The wind
is a coyote
on a hill
howling
for its family.

*Erin
Age 7*

The March wind
is a witch
swooping by you,
cackling
and screaming
in your ear.

*Brett
Age 8*

MARCH

March packs leaves
   sticks,
      paper and litter,
         and takes them away
           for a windy ride.

*Kathy
Age 11*

Spring is a singing month!

Matthew
Age 8

Spring is a bird with a worm!

Bobbie
Age 10

I heard a bird sing.
I saw a crocus grow.
Spring is coming —
   I told you so!

Diana
Age 7

A chirp of a bird
Fills the cool spring air.
A solemn breeze
Carries it through
The mountain peaks,
Through a lemon sunset.

Carol
Age 11

Spring brings
   bright new blossoms,
   pretty trees,
   and flowers.
Spring brings water, birds,
And lots of children
To play!

April
Age 6

Spring is playtime for the flowers
   showing off their colors.
Spring is when the wind has a tea party.
Spring is Mother Nature
   getting out her paintbrush.
Spring is a long wait!

Kathy
Age 11

See what I found . . .
   a baby bird . . .
   a baby bird that I will take care of . . .
   a baby bird I can love . . .
   a baby bird that will grow
      to be a big, brown bird . . .
   a baby bird to fly away.

Keith
Age 8

When I hear the wind
It makes me think
Of a bird
Flying
Faster and faster . . .

Chris
Age 10

Wind is a baby bird
Gliding
In the sky,
Flying away
Until spring is near.

Kristen
Age 8

Spring means a new bird nest
　in the apple tree!

　　　　Bob
　　　　Age 8

MARCH
Powerful, strong
Blows happy conversations!

　　　　Todd
　　　　Age 8

The blossom trees
　are soft and cuddly —
Like giant pillows.

　　　　Ben
　　　　Age 6

A nest is made of odds 'n ends
Candy wrappers
A piece of kite string —
But perfect for small sparrows.

　　　　Julie
　　　　Age 11

A rainbow is a fairy's bridge
With colors for cables.

　　　　Jeff
　　　　Age 10

THE RAIN
I hope it will not kill my plants,
Or even flood the poor little ants.

　　　　Bobbie
　　　　Age 10

SPRING RAIN
An umbrella and
　a straw hat
Go chatting
　together.

　　　　Mitzi
　　　　Age 11

SPRINGTIME
When flowers bloom and green appears
People laugh and shed no tears.
Blossoms burst, birds sing in tune,
There's love around from night till noon.
Butterflies with light wings fly
Up into the cloudless sky.
When spring arrives, the world is gay
With happiness from day to day.

　　　　Cathleen
　　　　Age 10

PUSSY WILLOWS
Pussy willow, pussy willow,
Where do you live?
　On a tree
　On a bush
　Or in a flower bed?

　　　　Trent
　　　　Age 6

46

Spring is singing in the sun!

Zachary
Age 6

SPRING SHOWER

A little bit of wind
A little bit of rain
And a little bit of wetness
   on my little windowpane.

Jocelyn
Age 11

If I could be the rain
I'd get the whole world wet and soggy!

Todd
Age 7

LIGHTNING

Like a giant spark
It lights up the dark.
It causes damage
That is hard to manage.

Dean
Age 10

RAIN

It's raining today.
It's raining so hard.
It's been raining so long
I can't play out in our yard.

Sue
Age 11

People walk around
Splashing silver on their boots,
Then lightning breaks it into designs
And makes a beautiful rainbow!

Paul
Age 7

RAINBOW

A cataract of color going to and fro!

Clark
Age 10

The rainbow is the angel's slippery slide.

Jennifer

RAINBOWS

Rainbows at the beginning of time
Were touched by the paintbrushes of heaven.
With the yellows as bright as the sun,
Its beam of light
Makes the pot of gold
At the end.

Barbara
Age 10

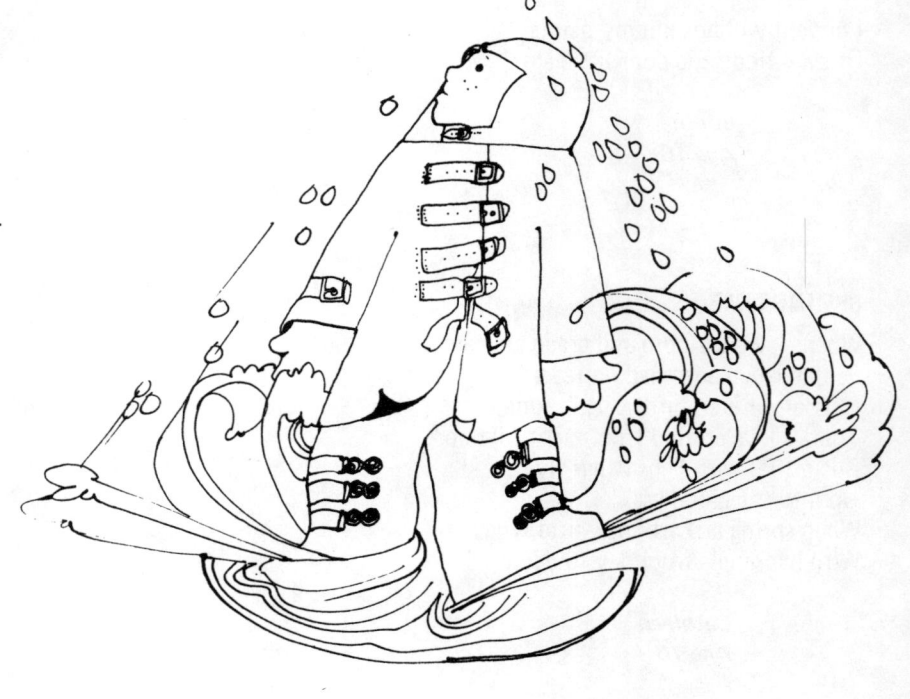

SPRING

I feel like blooming
just like a flower!

*Dean
Age 10*

Snow is melting
Leaves are appearing
New life begins.

*Tom
Age 10*

Clouds at night are pink cotton candy
Moving with the wind.

*Rhonda
Age 9*

Spring is going without a coat!

*Guy
Age 9*

SPRING IS...

A lot of flowers
All snuggled up together
Like they are getting cold.

Debbie

FLOWER

Bud closed up tightly
There's no key to unlock it —
Then it blossoms out.

*Carol
Age 9*

Spring is everywhere.
Pollen is in the air.
Breezes share the dandelion
While I send Kleenex tissues flying!

*Edwin
Age 11*

Once-A-Year Days

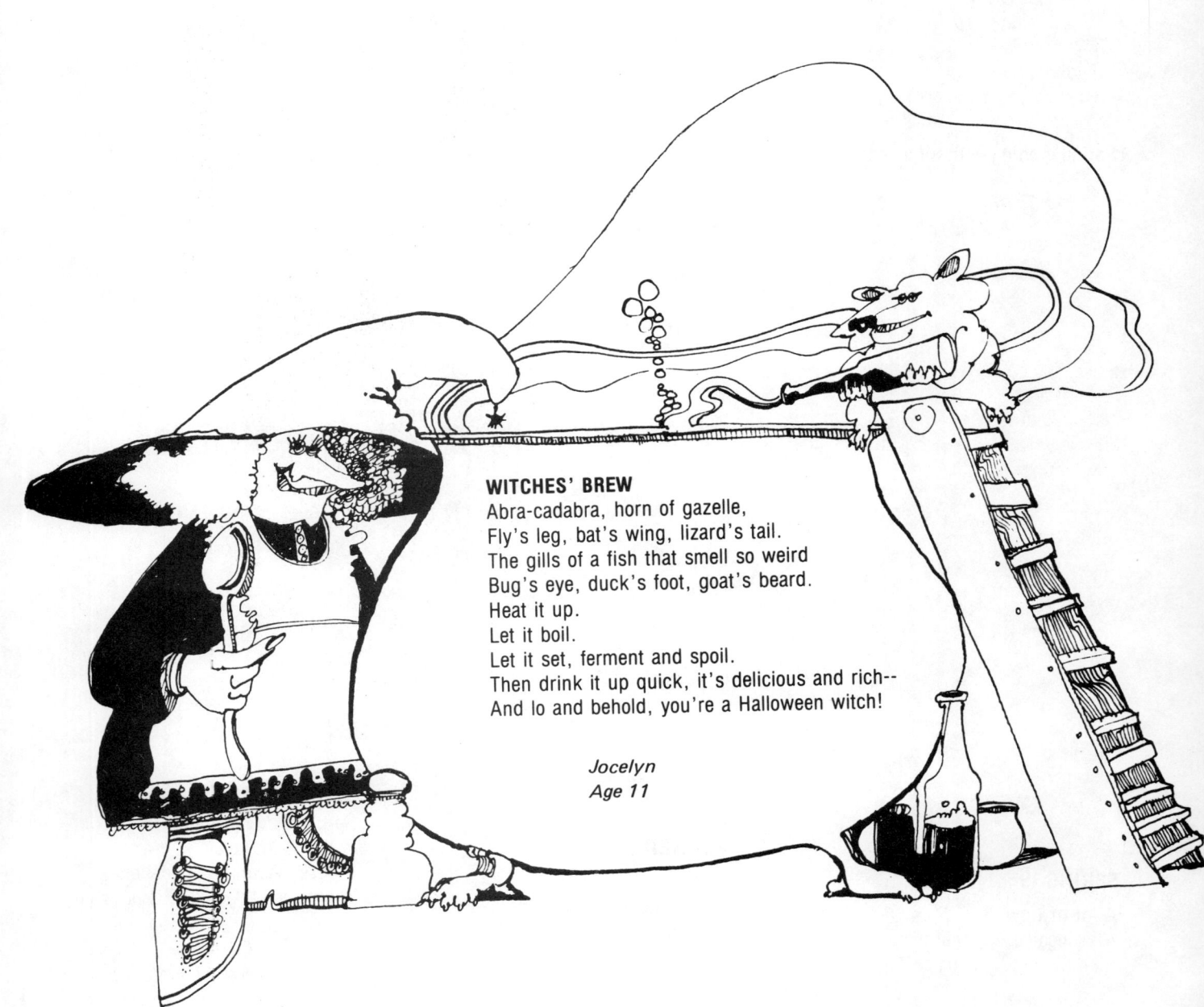

WITCHES' BREW

Abra-cadabra, horn of gazelle,
Fly's leg, bat's wing, lizard's tail.
The gills of a fish that smell so weird
Bug's eye, duck's foot, goat's beard.
Heat it up.
Let it boil.
Let it set, ferment and spoil.
Then drink it up quick, it's delicious and rich--
And lo and behold, you're a Halloween witch!

Jocelyn
Age 11

HALLOWEEN

At night
   when the wind is howling
   and the witches are flying
   and the pumpkins sit out
   and watch

At night
   when the huge yellow moon
   blows
Just watch out for the wind!

Jennifer
Age 9

Thanksgiving is
   lots of rolls
   and cranberry sauce —
   and when grandmas and aunties
   are the boss!

Michelle
Age 9

Midnight is
   when a black sheet of wool
   covers the world.

Stacey
Age 9

Thanksgiving is
   sitting in the kitchen
   while your mom and dad
   eat in the dining room with company.

Ellen
Age 9

HALLOWEEN

It's Halloween —
   let's have a party.
We'll invite Kim, Sue, Jane,
   and Marty.
We'll be ghosts and goblins
   and witches to scare you,
You can make a spook alley
   and scare us, too.
We'll scream and then scare everyone
And have lots and lots of scary fun!

Shanna
Age 9

THANKSGIVING

My brother is pot-bellied,
   Of course he's only three,
But at Thanksgiving
There's no one as fat
   as Grandfather and me!

Elizabeth
Age 9

CHRISTMAS

Christmas is a time of joy
With wonderful scents, feelings and sights.
I smell mint and pine.
I see a Christmas tree, all aglow
But most of all I feel the
Warmth of the Christmas Spirit.

Michelle
Age 9

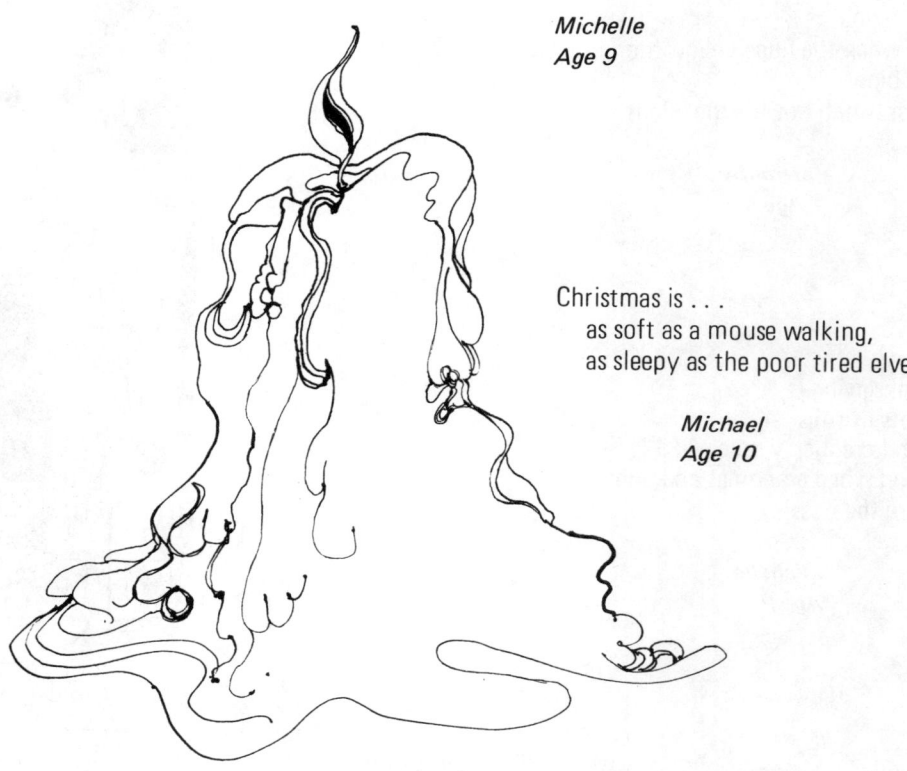

It came upon
   a stormy night.
The stars were shining
   very bright.
The pines were
   letting out their scent,
As if they knew
   what Christmas meant.
Then came a new
   and shiny morn,
When the sun
   was very warm.
You should have seen
   the pretty sight,
By long, last flickering
   candlelight.

Sharon
Age 9

Christmas is . . .
   as soft as a mouse walking,
   as sleepy as the poor tired elves.

Michael
Age 10

Christmas is
Jesus born in the stable
With the animals gathered around
The new King.
Christmas is love.

Theresa
Age 10

CANDLE

On the table
In the corner
A waxed, knarled, wrinkled old man —
Memories of losses and gains
Flickering in his eye.
His tears flow down
As he melts with old age and use,
Dripping.

Anne
Age 11

CHRISTMAS

Children like Christmas
How do I know?
Ribbons and bows
Iced cookies and snow.

Santa Claus, presents
Trees all aglow.
Mom and dads
All on the go.

Patricia
Age 10

CANDLE

A small flame whose light is dim.
It peeps like an eager child
Who quietly steals down the stairway
To watch the party in silent rapture.

Julianne
Age 11

Christmas is on its way.
  The sparkling lights
   Glow at night.
Ornaments hang so gay.
  The presents shine.
  One is MINE.

Michelle
Age 9

Christmas is as old as Santa's wife!

Steve
Age 10

CHRISTMAS THOUGHTS

Christmas is
Jesus born in the stable
And presents under the tree.
Christmas is
Getting excited,
Christmas is
Giving love to one another.

Tracy
Age 10

My favorite place
On the bough is where
The silver bells shine,
The stars twinkle,
And the ornaments glow.

Stacey
Age 9

Peppermint candy canes hang
   on evergreen boughs
As the dazzling tree twirls around.
Crimson presents glisten;
Crystal bells chime.
Glowing candles melt sending wax flowing down
   like a glassy river waking up
      to the wintery air.

Julie
Age 10

A dove upon a golden chariot —
Flies.
Ebony thoughts lie sleeping —
Waiting.
Silent eyes will awake
At dawn
To presents and ornaments
Filled with angelic crimson.

Liane
Age 11

Christmas is
White snow
With delicious cookies
For Santa.
Christmas is
Giving presents away.

Denice
Age 10

Christmas is
opening the present
you wanted two years ago.

Debra
Age 9

Now that Christmas is over,
It makes me feel sad
Because all the pretty boxes
And paper get wasted.

Rob
Age 10

REGRETS

I'd like to dance or sing a song.
I'd like to dive or run along.
I'd like just one more candy cane —
If I just didn't have this pain.

Michael
Age 9

A PINE CANDLE

Watch it . . .
It stands alone
Like the last light
On St. Nicholas Eve.
Its light glowing
It seems to see
All who sit around it.

Lisa
Age 11

ST. PATRICK'S DAY

Leprechauns, leprechauns,
  and pots of gold.
Leprechauns, leprechauns,
Do they never grow old?
I dream and I dream
  of little green men.
I dream and I dream —
  but I never catch them!

Michelle
Age 11

February is the month
When love is sent around!

Mark
Age 7

Now that
Christmas is over
All the presents
Are opened
And scattered around.
The house is boring.
You have to wait another year.

Ronda
Age 10

EASTER BUNNY

Here comes the Easter bunny
Hopping down his trail.
If he can't get it to your house,
He'll send it through the mail.

Elwin
Age 11

EASTER TIME

Easter is a special time,
Our Lord was crucified.
On the cross he hung by nails
And very painfully died.

Now he will always reign,
And there will be no doom
For on that joyful Easter morning
He was risen from the tomb.

Heidi
Age 11

The day before Easter
My teacher said to me:
"The chocolate bunny you can have,
The Easter eggs go to me."

Glen
Age 11

APRIL FOOLS!

I heard a cat start barking,
I heard a dog meow.
I saw a fish start walking
And my friend act like a cow.

I saw a horse start flying,
I saw rocks turn into jewels.
Then suddenly it hit me . . .
Today is April Fools!

Barbara
Age 11

Happiness is having a new long dress and rabbits.

Anita
Age 7

ALL IN ONE DAY

White bunnies hopping and playing
Hiding colored eggs.
And in the morning you find them,
And roll them down a sand hill
And then eat them afterward.
(But you have to wash them, first.)
And all your relatives have fun
At a big Easter dinner.
Then bedtime.
But the next morning —
You want to do the same thing
All over again.

Kerry
Age 11

Easter is horrible.
You have to get all dressed up
For a whole day!

Georgene
Age 10

From Mt. Olympus

Olympus
Gods' palace
Kept Gods safe
Palace surrounded by clouds
Olympus

Terry
Age 7

Prosperpine
Kind, beautiful,
She was caught
By pale, cold Pluto.

Diana
Age 7

Apollo
Dazzling sunburst
Flaming chariot flies
God of the sun!

Lee

Ceres
Beautiful goddess
  of the harvest.
She was tender.
Golden Ceres!

Staci

Pandora
Beautiful, lovely
Opened the jar
Curiosity caused us evil.

Diana
Age 7

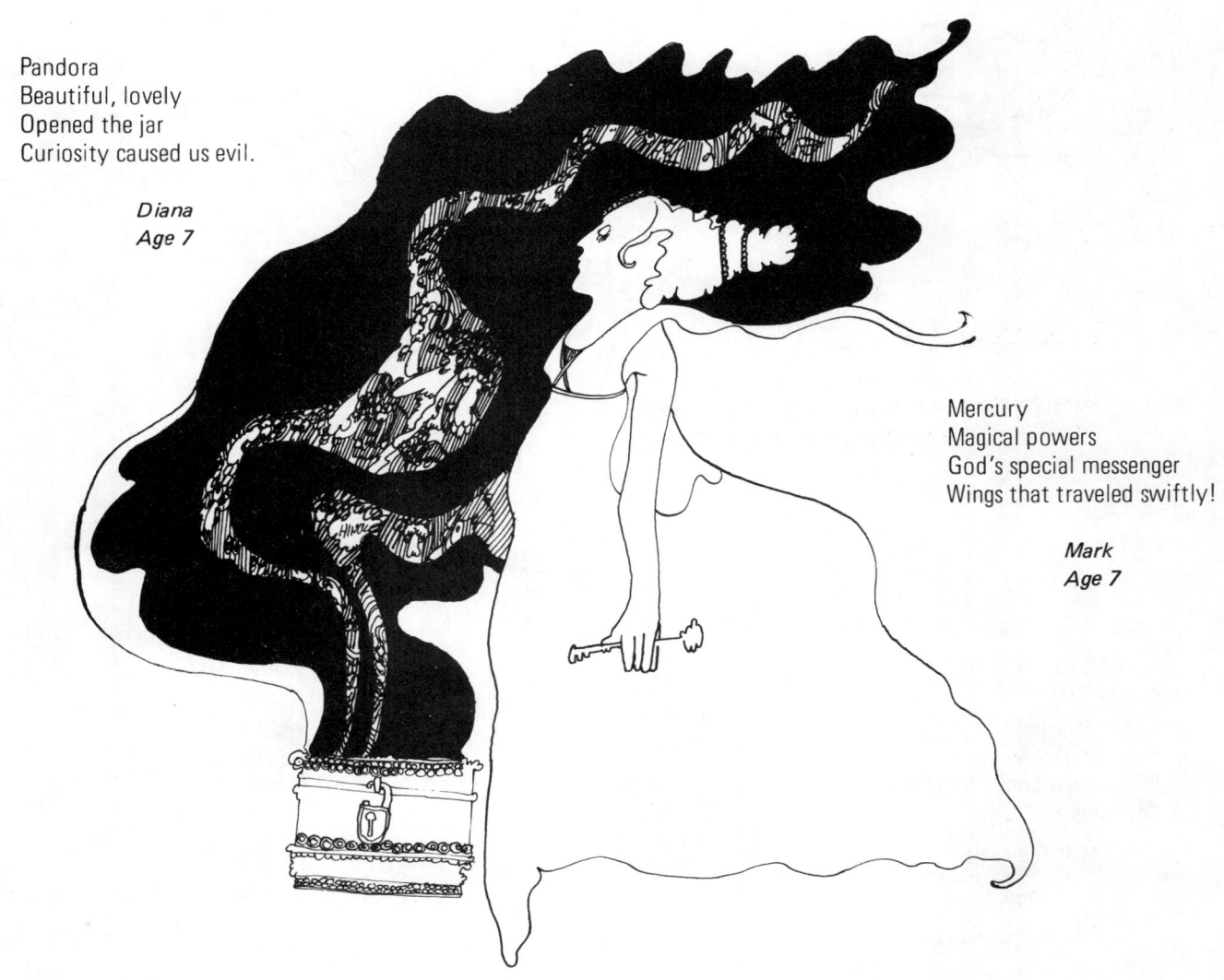

Mercury
Magical powers
God's special messenger
Wings that traveled swiftly!

Mark
Age 7

In My Crayon Box

BLUE IS MY FAVORITE COLOR

Blue is a lake by a mountain
Blue is the water from a fountain.
Blue is the sky, oh, so high.
Blue is the color of clothes I wear
Blue is not the color of hair.
Blue is my crayon in a box
Blue is a frame on the clocks.
Blue is a poster hanging on my wall,
Blue is the color of our school hall.

Peggy
Age 10

RED

Fire engines are scarlet
Rainbows are rosy
Flags and birds are cardinal
Ribbons are lobster
Shirts are castilian
Roses and cherries and
Apples are rubies!

*Scott
Age 9*

A crayon is a little man on one stilt.

*Suzanne
Age 7*

Purple is a plum that hangs from a tree under the silent sunset.

*Vickie
Age 9*

BLUE

Blue is the sky
   breaking into an orange sunset.
Blue is the ocean
   reaching toward the shore.
Blue is the mournful cry of a baby.
Blue is the mountain
   at the end of a day.
Blue is midnight loneliness.

*Lory
Age 11*

Purple is the inside
   of a kitten's ear,
A streak of a rainbow
   after rain,
Purple is a gentle color
   in a silent dream.

*Andrea
Age 9*

BLACK IS...

Black is the sadness of my heart
Black is the darkness of the night
Black is like dying on a rainy day
Black is hate

*Terry
Age 11*

GREEN SCENE

Green is the color of a lime,
Green is the color of the pants
   of mine.
Green is the grass so tall
Green are the leaves that fall.
Green is the carpet
Green is the grass
Green is the color
   of a movie pass.
Green is the color
   of a tweedle bug.
Green is the color of our shag rug.

*Cheryl
Age 10*

PINK

Pink is the color of roses so gay.
Pink is fragrance far away.
Pink is the color of sweaters and skirts.
Pink is the color of my undershirts.
Pink is the color of rosy cheeks.
It is sometimes the color of bleach.

Wendy
Age 10

GREEN

Green is the color of some trees
Also blackboards, magic markers,
   and peas.
Green springtime is almost here,
When suddenly green grass
   will appear.
I like green, yes I do.
It's nature's most perfect hue!

Michelle
Age 11

Black is the night.
Black is a big shiny car.
Black is a tire as it rolls along.
Black is a bruise that hurts.

Robert
Age 7

Gray is the oatmeal I eat for breakfast.

Donald
Age 9

Brown is a monkey
   swinging through the trees
Brown is a bear
   pestering some bees.

Jimmy
Age 10

RED

Red is the color of a sunburned nose,
Red is the color of a beautiful rose.
Sometimes, red is very light.
Sometimes it's red, almost at night.
Red comes in more than one shade,
It all depends on the way it's made.
Red is a very good color —
I like to see it on my mother!

Tom
Age 10

PURPLE

The bubbles look purple in my huge pool,
And purple is my pencil at school.
Purple runs all around —
And a gurgle is its sound.
Purple can be dark.
It sounds like a seal's loud bark.
Purple can be light —
And purple is the sky at night.

Matthew
Age 7

GOLD

Gold is a happy day,
Waiting for a friend.
Gold is sending a letter
　　far away.

*Apryl
Age 10*

Red is a sunset showing
　in the sky,
Red is a cardinal flying by.
Red is the color of a pretty rose.
Red is the color of a sunburned nose.

*Kelly
Age 7*

RED IS...

Red is a firecracker —
　a fire engine
　　and your face when you're angry.

*Danny
Age 10*

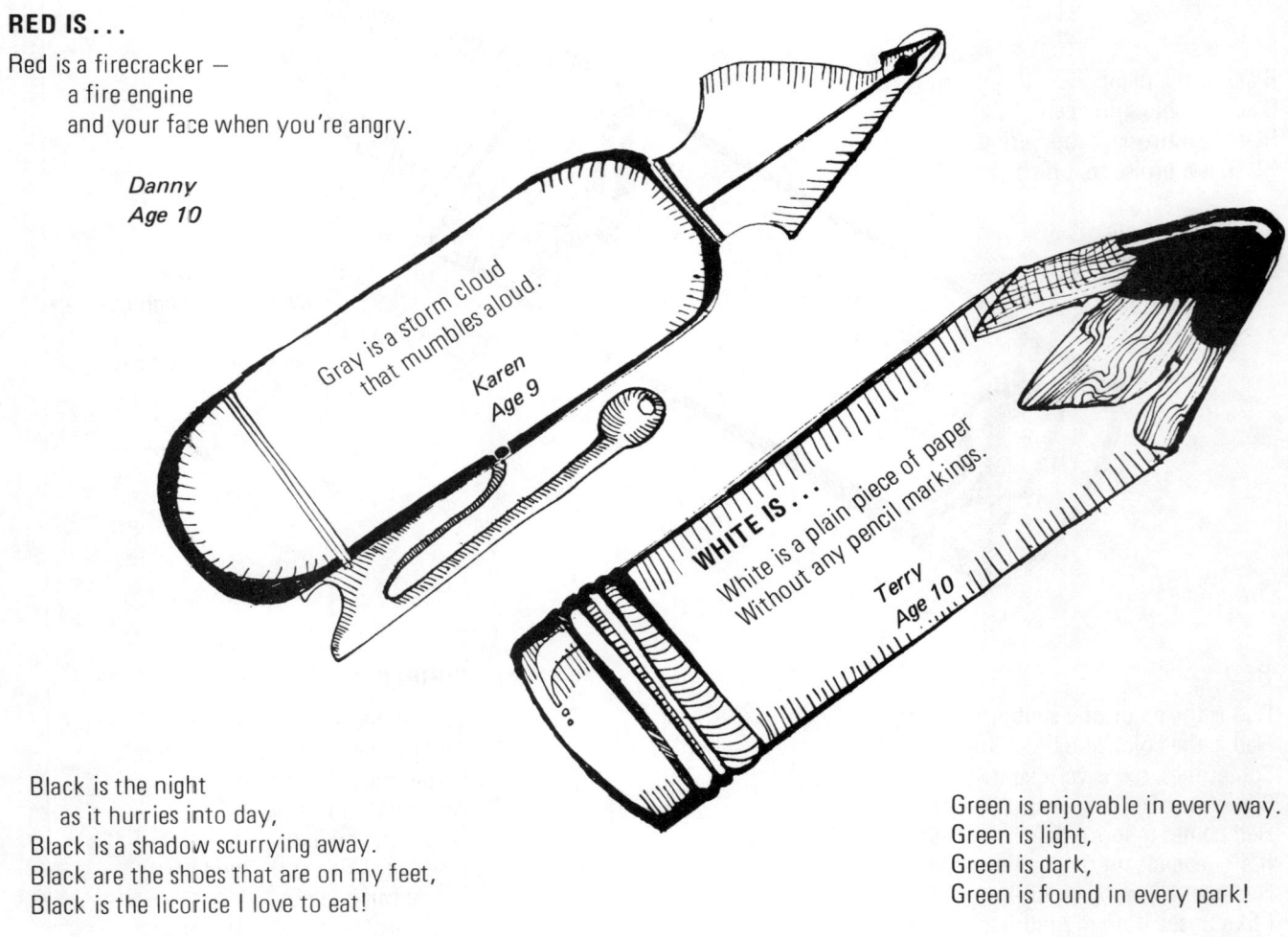

Gray is a storm cloud
that mumbles aloud.

*Karen
Age 9*

WHITE IS...

White is a plain piece of paper
Without any pencil markings.

*Terry
Age 10*

Black is the night
　as it hurries into day,
Black is a shadow scurrying away.
Black are the shoes that are on my feet,
Black is the licorice I love to eat!

*Susan
Age 10*

Green is enjoyable in every way.
Green is light,
Green is dark,
Green is found in every park!

*Adrian
Age 11*

RED

Red is a heart trimmed with lace,
Red is the color of an embarrassed face.
Red is the love shared with others,
Red are the roses we send to our mothers!

Debra
Age 9

PURPLE

Purple is a violet
I gave to my mom.
Purple is love.
Purple can make you sing.
Purple is joy —
Purple is being alone.

Jackie
Age 10

I think gray is lonely —
It reminds me of tired, ugly buildings
And old, lonely, gray-haired people.

Black is the color of Halloween night.
It's also Tim's eyes
(When we're in a fight.)

Bart
Age 10

RED IS...

Red is a strawberry,
Juicy and sweet.
Red is a feeling
All warm and complete.
Red is an Indian standing high.
Red is a hot cherry pie!

Tracie
Age 10

BLUE

Blue is the color of my eyes,
Blue is the color of the skies.
Blue is the color of pen ink,
Blue is very different from pink.
Blue is breathing in fresh air —
I wish blue were everywhere!

Glenn
Age 11

YELLOW

Yellow is the sun on a bright summer day,
Yellow is a baby chick playing in the hay.
Yellow is a pansy with green leaves on its stem,
Yellow is my brother's cake, he just turned ten.

Teresa
Age 10

City Scenes

CITY LIFE

A city is my place to be
With crowded cars and buildings.
The smog, the fumes,
The sweet perfumes
Give way to city life.

Todd
Age 11

The little old shack is sitting by the stream.
Nestled in the shade it stands
Waiting for a friend.

    Bret
    Age 9

The grinning house
   has leaves swishing all over —
Red, yellow, orange, and brown
Whispering secrets to each other
   that no one can understand.

    Becky
    Age 9

Reflections in the sun
Looking through waffle-clouds
Watching the sunrise.

    Paul
    Age 7

My house
Your house
Everybody's house.
His house
Her house
Does it have a mouse?
Cat's house
Dog's house
Do they always fight?
My house
Your house
Are they always bright?

    Rebecca
    Age 9

Ghost towns
   Tumbleweeds
      Broken houses
Sand castles
   Tall and smooth
Wind blows the sand
   It disappears
      Gone
      Vanished
Does it matter?

    Donna
    Age 11

A dirty, old house is sitting
   in the brown grass.
Plants dry and droop
   toward the ground.
I look at them and think
   how lovely they once were.

    Shannon
    Age 9

Cross - Stitchery

THE NUMBER SEVEN

S is for sea lions
    that swim in the sea,
E is for eagles
    who nest in a tree.
V is for Victor
    who lives next to me,
E is for elephants
    who romp happily.
N is for the nice things
    seven can be!

Leslie Ann
Age 10

J olly
I mportant
M idget!

Jim
Age 9

R un
O ver
B ob
E xcept
R emember the
T ruth.

Robert
Age 10

S hame on you,
H enry and
A nn! You broke a window and
R an! Whose?
O urs! Why you
N aughty kids!

Sharon
Age 10

R uth
U sually
T ries to
H ide from her mom.

Ruth
Age 10

CATS

C ats climb!
A ct up and
T rack mud!

Juliana
Age 8

This Is My Country

MY COUNTRY

This is my country, my home.
This is where freedom flows out
And love glows within.
This is where I was born;
This is where I will die.
This is where I am happy,
Even through hard times.
This is where justice is
And will forever remain.
This is where we have understanding.
This is where we are thankful,
This is the land of plenty.
This is where our flag blows free.
This is my country!

Robyn
Age 10

RED, WHITE, AND BLUE

The red stands for freedom,
White for pride,
And the blue for the songs of anthem.

> *Sonja*
> *Age 10*

1865

Blue reminds me of marching soldiers
In their uniforms all ragged and worn.
I walk along watching them,
Wondering which uniform I'll wear . . .

> *Joey*
> *Age 10*

AMERICA

America the beautiful
America the free.
America the wonderful
I pledge my heart to thee.

The land that you were built upon
Was touched by God's own hand.
From the forests and mountains and timber land
To the beaches filled with sand.

America the beautiful,
America the free.
America the wonderful —
I pledge my life to thee.

> *Norman*
> *Age 11*

FREEDOM

Freedom is to worship God
In your own way.
Freedom is to go where you please
And stand
And say
What you feel!

> *Debra*
> *Age 10*

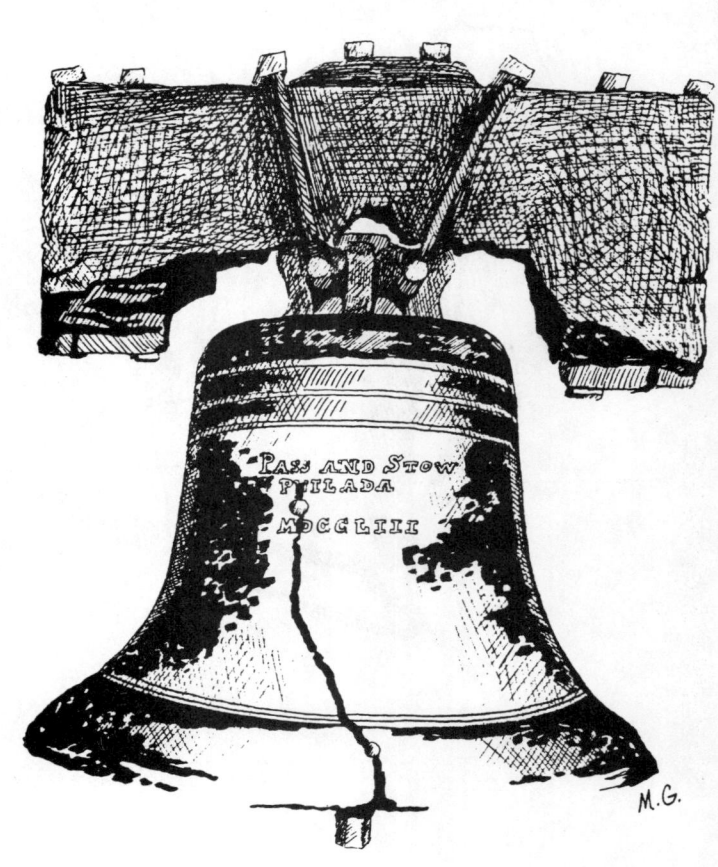

Hopscotch Math

I like to mix,
I like to fix.
10 - 4 = 6.

*Anita
Age 7*

Open the window,
Shut the door,
12 + 12 = 24.

*Chris
Age 7*

I have homework,
It's not done.
3 x 7 = 21.

*Belinda
Age 11*

6 x 1 = 6
My coughdrops
Were Vicks!

*Staci
Age 7*

Hurry, hurry,
You are late!
4 + 4 = 8.

*Paul
Age 7*

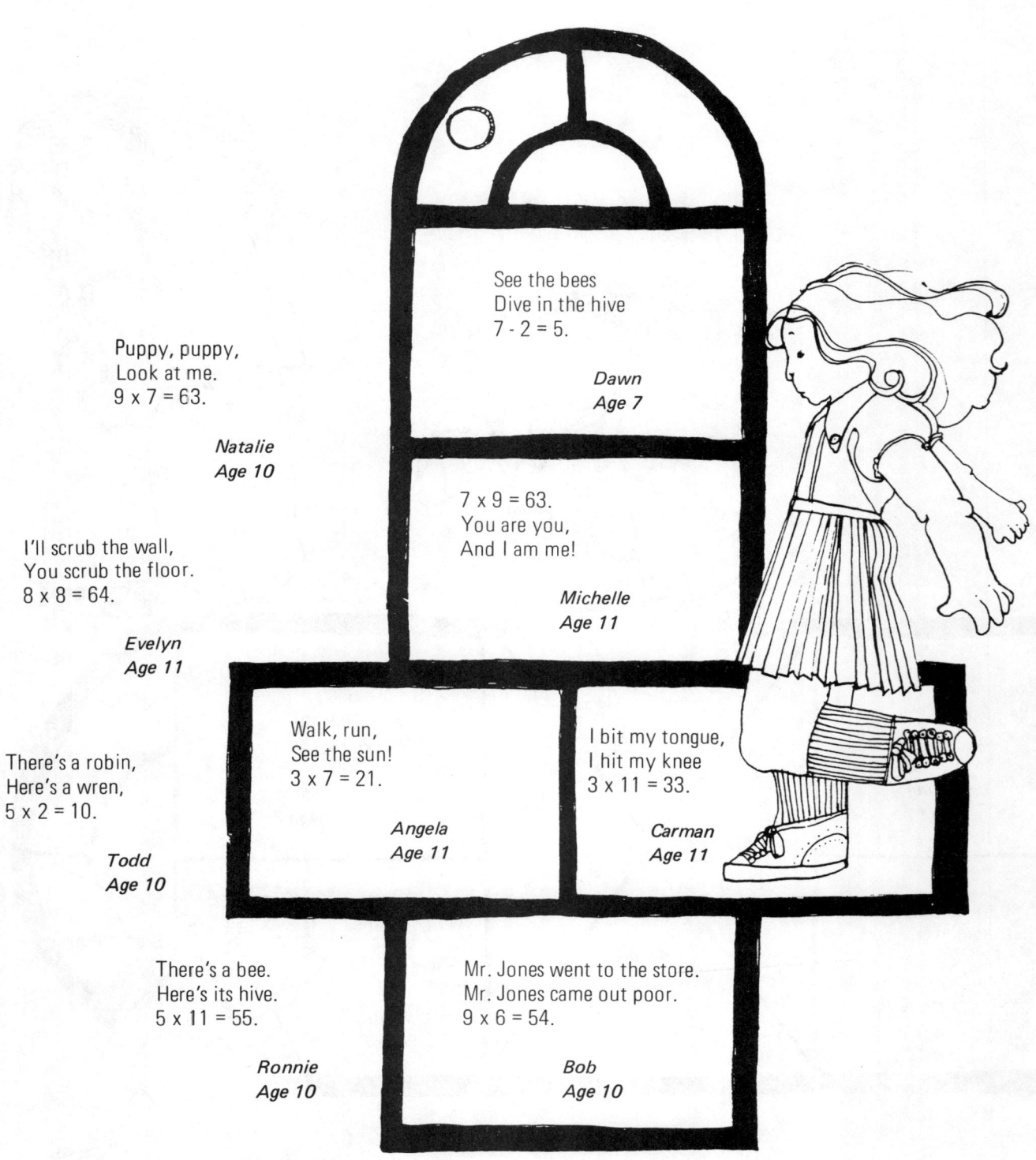

Puppy, puppy,
Look at me.
9 x 7 = 63.

*Natalie
Age 10*

I'll scrub the wall,
You scrub the floor.
8 x 8 = 64.

*Evelyn
Age 11*

There's a robin,
Here's a wren,
5 x 2 = 10.

*Todd
Age 10*

See the bees
Dive in the hive
7 - 2 = 5.

*Dawn
Age 7*

7 x 9 = 63.
You are you,
And I am me!

*Michelle
Age 11*

Walk, run,
See the sun!
3 x 7 = 21.

*Angela
Age 11*

I bit my tongue,
I hit my knee
3 x 11 = 33.

*Carman
Age 11*

There's a bee.
Here's its hive.
5 x 11 = 55.

*Ronnie
Age 10*

Mr. Jones went to the store.
Mr. Jones came out poor.
9 x 6 = 54.

*Bob
Age 10*

Circus Sounds

CIRCUS

The drums will start rolling
The barker's eyes glowing
He says, "Having fun is the game!"
When the fat lady smiles,
It brings people from miles
For no circus is the same.

Behind the big curtain,
The clowns, they are certain
That people will laugh at their fun.
The horses are prancing
And ladies are dancing
While the barker puts in a small pun.

Then all will soon stop
And children's eyes pop
For the man on the high wire act.
The man pretends dizzy,
The screamers are busy;
The kids have a small heart attack.

But he makes it through safely
And poor little Katie
Says goodbye to the fun circus clown.
For the circus is over;
The next stop is Dover.
Next year, they'll be back in our town!

Carol Ann
Age 11

What would it be like to be a clown?
Would I always smile?
Would I ever frown?
Would I be very funny, by any chance?
Would I be able to scare
With one little glance?
Would I be in a circus?
Would I jump up and down?
What would it be like to be a clown?

James
Age 11

Acting funny,
In front of a crowd.
Shouting your feelings
Right out loud.

Under the smile,
No one knows you may frown.
Brush away the tear
'Cause you're a clown.

Sally
Age 12

A CLOWN

Why does a clown wear a frown?
Does he smile up and down?
Does he really care
  Or does he walk away?
What about the tear that falls,
  Is it fear or fun?
Why can't his heart be kind,
Just like the face he wears?

Julie
Age 11

The clown loves the crowd,
But is he happy or sad?
Is it all just makeup or real?
No one seems to know how clowns feel.

Tim
Age 11

Mr. Clown, who seems so gay
Just one question, if I may.
Acting so funny every day —
Is it work or is it play?

Patti
Age 11

Cats, Camels, And Caterpillars

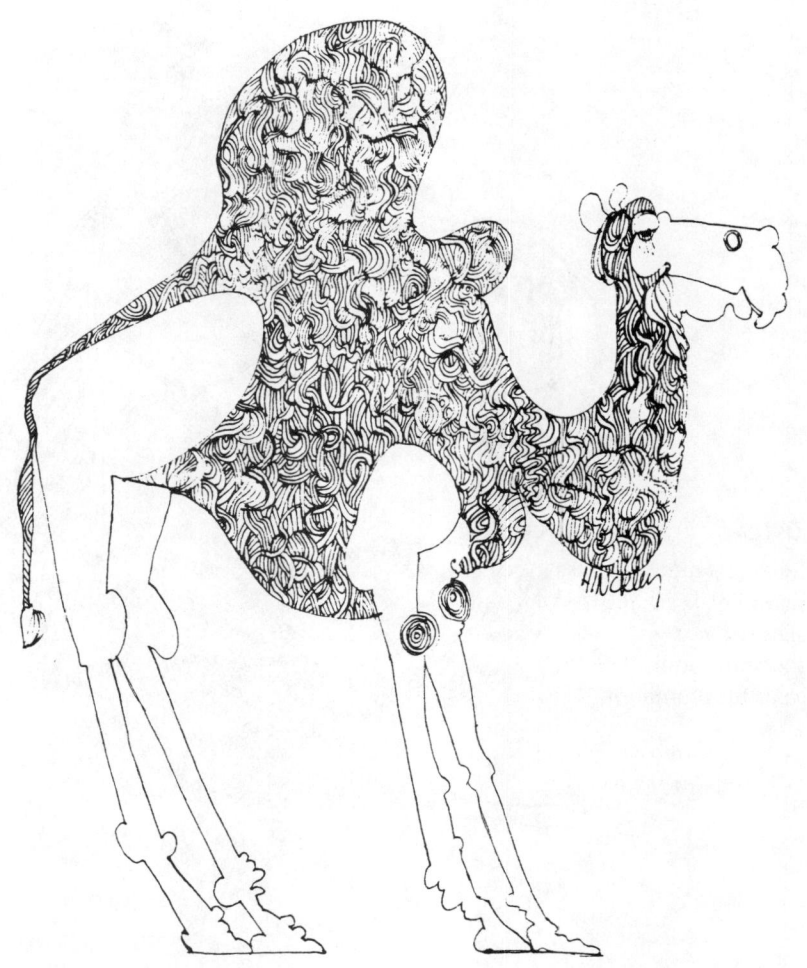

A soft fluffy cat
Sits quietly in a chair
Dreaming of white mice.

*Dennis
Age 9*

Baby cats
   are soft as a friend
     and snuggly as love.

*Natalie
Age 6*

CRICKETS

Pitch-black
Clicking, clacking legs
Blowing away in the wind
Crickets hopping on the logs.

*Ryan
Age 6*

THE CAMEL

Native in the blazing wilderness
The never-thirsting nomad wanders
Free from the world of men.

*Jocelyn
Age 11*

CATERPILLAR

Caterpillar
Fuzzy worm
Inching, squatting, crawling
Milkweed, food, pupa, cocoon
Spinning, changing, covering —
POP, flapping
Butterfly!

*Kalani
Age 11*

BEST FRIEND

He thanks me in the usual way —
A friendly wag of the tail.

Chris
Age 11

A grizzly bear
King of all,
Standing with majesty
On his jagged cliff —
Paws outstretched,
Head held high
Showing that this is his land!

Jill
Age 11

THE OWL

The owl is a gentleman
Of down-right fascination.
He opens his eyes
And shuts his mouth,
And gains his reputation!

Lorrie
Age 11

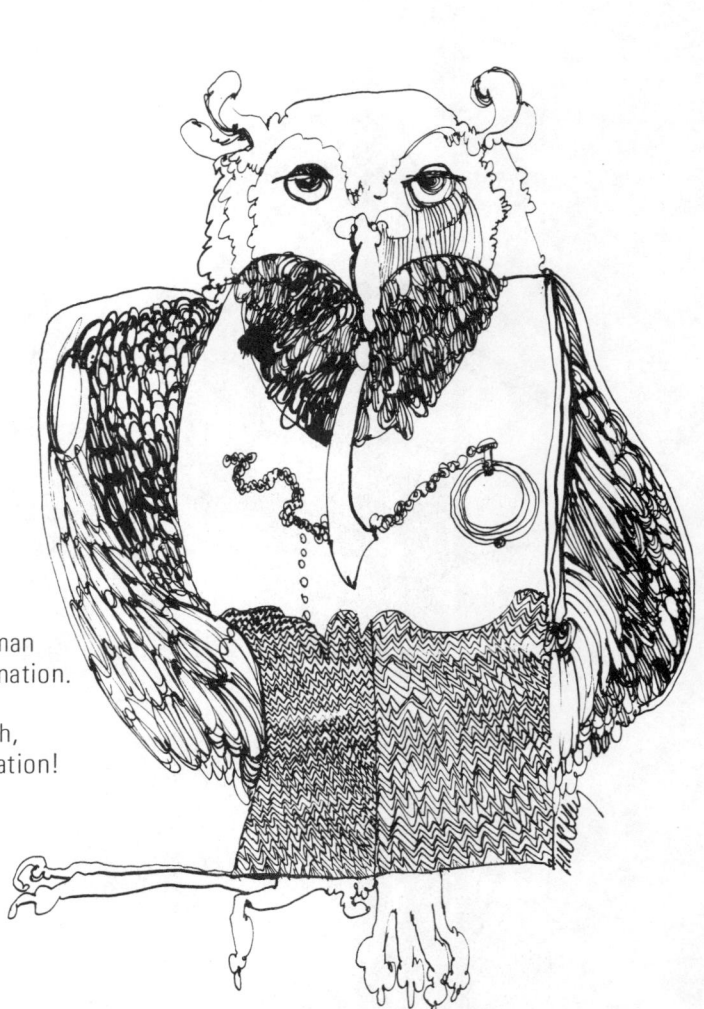

THE CROCODILE

The "gator" has a huge head,
And very sharp teeth, too.
His jaws clamp down when he is fed,
And there isn't a trace of you!
But my favorite is the crocodile,
The big, mean, nasty ones
That live on the banks of the River Nile,
Where out of people they have their fun.
His skin is tougher than silver armor,
His teeth are six-inches long.
Of death he is a wicked farmer,
And he croaks a wicked song.
He floats down streams like a hollow log
Until he finds unsuspecting prey.
But alas! This time it's only a frog
Who quickly swims away!

Barry
Age 11

HORSEBACK RIDING

Clip, clop, clip, clop.
My legs rub against the smooth saddle.
I ride up, down, up, down.
His coat is as black as the night.
His muscles are working,
Showing how strong he is.
Up, down, up, down —
As fast as the wind
I bounce, high on the back of my horse!

Robin
Age 9

Mother Ghost Rhymes

Hey diddle, diddle!
The ghost with the fiddle,
The monster jumped over the moon;
The goblin laughed
To see such a sight,
And the witch ran away in the night!

Sherri
Age 9

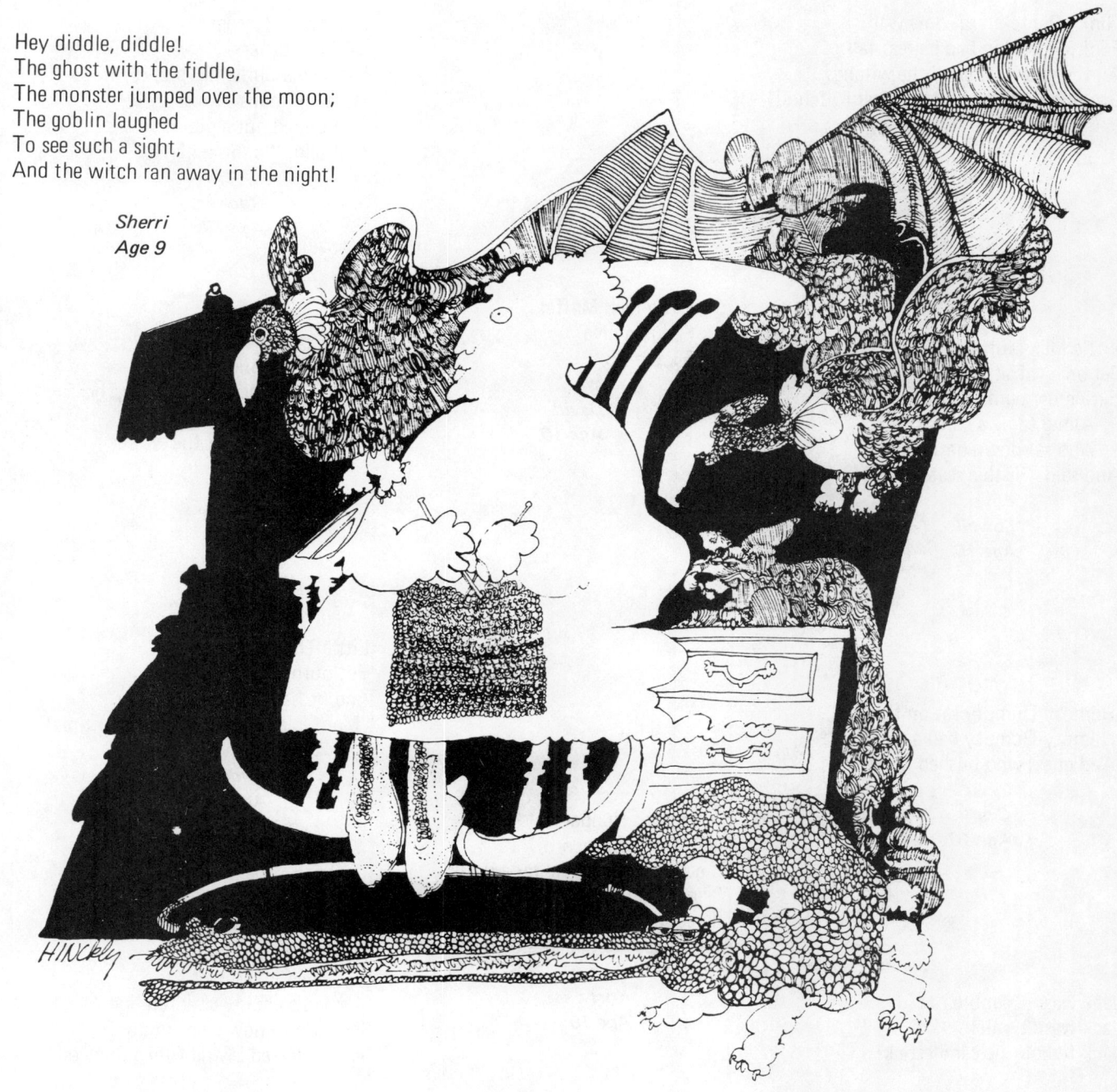

Punky Pumpkin sat on a wall.
Punky Pumpkin had a great fall.
All the goblins and all the witches
Got pumpkin pie all over their britches!

Shauna
Age 9

Little Miss Muffett
Sat on a tuffet,
Eating her curds and whey.
   Along came a spider
   Who sat down beside her
And said, "Is this seat taken?"

Lowell
Age 10

Little Miss Muffet
Fell in a hive
5 x 5 = 25.

David
Age 10

Humpty Dumpty sat on the wall,
Humpty Dumpty had a great fall;
And guess who pushed him?

Cindy
Age 10

Old Mother Hubbard
Went to the cupboard,
To get her poor daughter a dress;
When she got there
The cupboard was bare,
And so was her daughter, I guess.

Kort
Age 10

Jack wasn't nimble.
Jack wasn't quick.
Jack fell on the candlestick!

Paige
Age 10

Little Jack Horner
Sat in a corner
Eating his Christmas pie;
He stuck in his thumb,
And pulled out a plum,
And said, "Is this all I get?"

Rocky
Age 10

Peter, Peter pumpkin eater,
Had a wife and couldn't keep her;
Put her in a bottle . . .
And stored her for the winter.

Sonya
Age 10

Little Tom Tinker
Got burned on a clinker;
And he began to cry,
"Mom, Mom! that's the second time!"

Andrea
Age 10

THE OLD WOMAN IN THE SHOE

There was an old lady
Who lived in a shoe.
She had so many children
She didn't know what to do,
So she started saving Green Stamps!

Arnie
Age 9

Lights in the Sky

The stars are bright.
A city of lights in the sky.

Roger
Age 11

Still . . .
Like a painted picture
With the reflection of a mountain
So hushed
So quiet
Without a ripple.
Still as a soundless sigh.

Denise
Age 11

THE MOON

Sailing in God's world
She's a round ball —
Silver in space.

Paul
Age 7

ASTRONAUT

Exploring the misty blue
He sees the unnoticed,
Finds the unseen
And discovers the unknown.

*Jocelyn
Age 11*

A falling star is a light bulb
Falling from the shattered sky above.

*Robert
Age 10*

Looking into the sky.
Imagining
   what's out there.
Wondering where.
Wondering why.

*Matt
Age 10*

S parkling
T winkling
A ncient
R adiant
S hining

*Pam
Age 10*

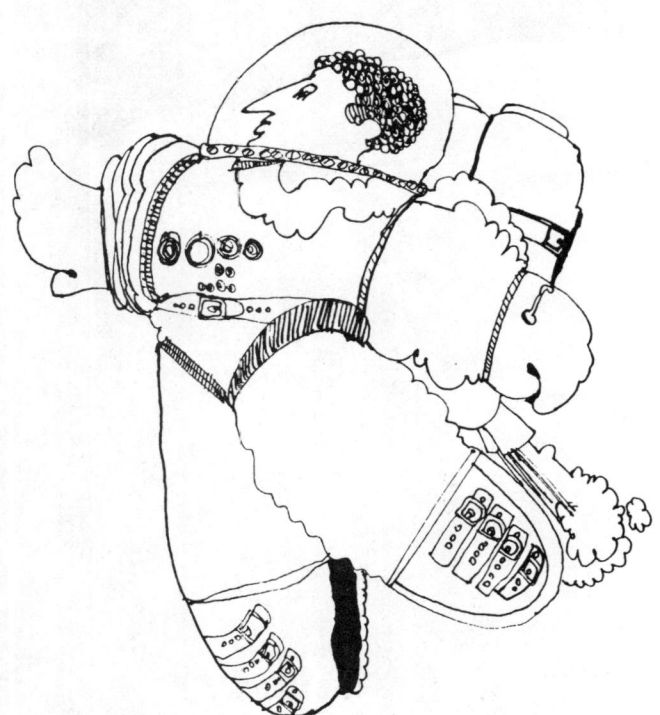

Stars in the sky
Shooting through the air
A nightly battle.

*Josh
Age 10*

STARS

Appearing.
Disappearing.
Twinkling.
Falling.
I can t reach their light.

*Mike
Age 7*

A rainbow is a ring of color.

*Jeff
Age 10*

JUPITER

I would like to go to Jupiter
Because it is the BIGGEST PLANET
   IN THE UNIVERSE!

*John
Age 7*

The earth spins in orbit
Moving right under my feet.
Changing night to day.

Suzy
Age 11

The universe is an eternal plain
With shiny rocks here and there.
It has no up.
It has no down.
It is without end —
It goes on forever.

Gordon
Age 9

Planets are such special things
They mean so much to me.
Can you tell by what I say,
I'm "hooked" on astronomy?

Russell
Age 11

The sun has a light switch
But no one turns out the light.
It dips and turns
And when it spins
It spills golden nice dreams over the world!

Paul
Age 11

The goal out there
Is like a live planet
Waiting there
For someone to live on it.
It is like a point of life.
Are you going to make it?

Kathy
Age 11

Limericks and Other Green Things

PEAS

Peas have a very strange taste.
When you squash them, they make a paste.
   I hate the smell,
     So it's just as well
That I let my peas go to waste.

      Tom
      Age 10

Miss Simple wears curls of green.
She looks horribly vicious and mean.
    And her brothers say —
    She dyed it today
With grasses and green vaseline.

      Sally
      Age 10

There was an old man named Blake
Who thought he could swallow a snake.
   When the snake went down,
   He thought it would drown;
But now, Blake has a bad tummy ache!

      David
      Age 11

JOLLY GREEN

A big green giant
  is on the label
    of the can
      of little peas.

      Gordon
      Age 9

THE FROG

Like a speckled rock
As still as a lifeless leaf
Polka-dotted frog.

      Andrew
      Age 9

Epitaphs

Here lies Horace
He sang with a chorus.
One day while eating some hay,
His voice and life drifted away.

*Cynthia
Age 10*

Below in this cupboard
Lies old Mother Hubbard.

*Tara
Age 11*

Here lies the bones
of poor old Sam
Folks say he died
'cause his wife was a nag

*Bretta
Age 11*

John was brave,
stalwart and wise.
He met his maker
with great surprise!

*Kim
Age 11*

Here lies the bones
of Janet.
She came from
an unknown planet.

*Janet
Age 11*

Here lies a man
Who happily died.
May God give him mercy
Because nobody cried.

*David
Age 10*

In this grave
Lies dangerous Dave.
He died because
He wouldn't behave.

*Steve
Age 11*

Here lies Mr. Platter
His death — historical matter

*Bart
Age 10*

Here lies Crystal
Shot by a pistol!

*Julie
Age 10*

DAVID BONE
1705
In this grave
Beneath this stone
Lies David Bone
So alone!

*Deanna
Age 10*

Little Miss Muffet
Died on her tuffet

*Kurt
Age 10*

Here lies the bones
of Jeffrey O. Klunk.
They say he died
while coming home drunk.

*Allison
Age 11*

Silly Sounding Sentences

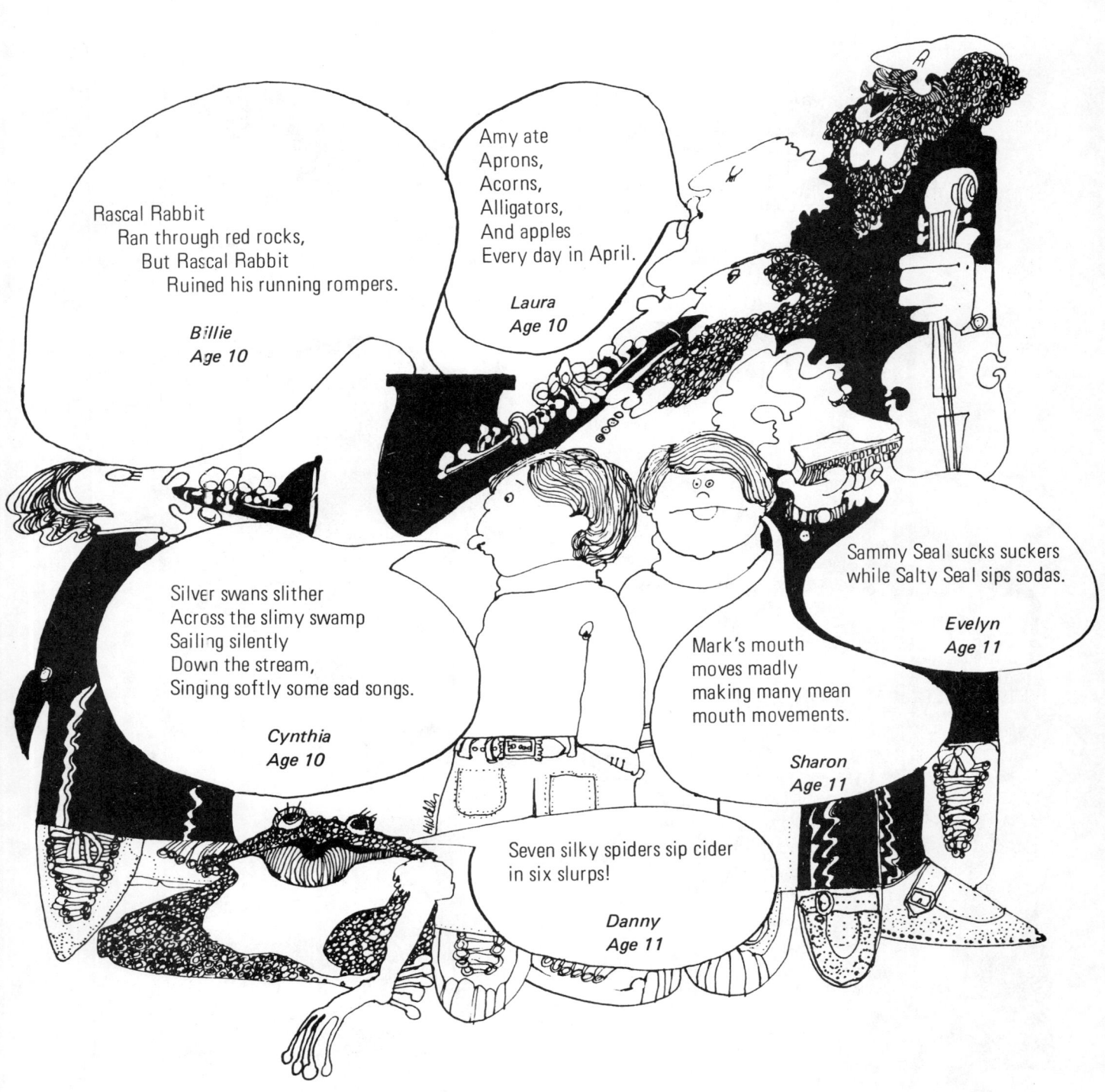

Poem Dust

HURRY

Hurry says the teacher,
Hand in your homework.
Hurry says the crossguard,
The light is red.
Hurry says the mother,
Now it's time for supper.
Hurry says the father,
Go get ready for bed.
Slowly says the night —
Rest your weary head.

*Terry
Age 10*

There was an old lady
Who saw an old horse.
He was carrying a bag,
Going golfing, of course.

*Devin
Age 7*

APPLES

Apples are good
Apples are bright
Apples don't spoil
Your "apple-tite!"

*Janice
Age 10*

There was an old lady
Who bought a few rhymes.
How much did they cost her?
Just a few dimes

*David
Age 7*

My friend Fred
Has raspberry freckles
And a strawberry head!

*Jeff
Age 9*

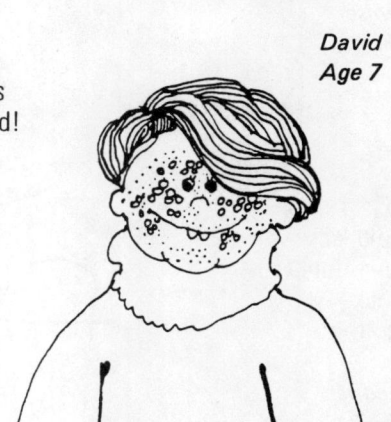

WORD OF THE DAY: SNOW

There once was a lady A-lab-a-cus Snow,
She went to the market, but she didn't know
Her baby boy dog was following low,
Was following Lady A-lab-a-cus Snow.
A-lab-a-cus Snow, she went to a show.
Her dog followed in, and still very low;
He ate all her popcorn until it was gone.
He ran out of the movie and stubbed his dog toe.
He ran out of the movies, ran out of the show.

*Brenda
Age 10*

MY MR. CHOOCHEEMOOCHEE

Far upon the chimney
Farther than I can see
There lives a little, silver man.
I call him Choocheemoochee.

He lives there still and silent
As quiet as can be.
Sometimes little birds visit
My Mr. Choocheemoochee.

On cold winter night,
From under his tin billows
A dozen or so clusters
Of big, black satin pillows.

Now look out the window
And see what you see.
I wonder if you can find
My Mr. Choocheemoochee.

Denise
Age 11

WHEELS

Bicycle wheels
sound
like music
when the wind
blows
through
the spokes.

Cathy
Age 10

There was an old lady
Who was rolling a ball.
She dropped it once
And it rolled down the hall.

Keith
Age 7

RASPBERRIES

Sit down dearies.
So I can tell about raspberries.
Some are sour,
Some are sweet,
But, I tell you they are a treat.
I love them!
I love them!
I really, honestly do.
I think I will even share one
    with you!

Brenda
Age 11

There was an old lady
Who played on a flute.
She gave it a kick
And made it go toot.

Jacque
Age 7

Bubbles
Sizzles
Packed in one.
Full of excitement
    and fizzles
Soda pop is lots of fun!

Mitzi
Age 11

OLD TRAIN
Blowing whistles echo
Through
Midnight darkness.
One glowing eye
Crawling back and forth
On silver webs,
Cutting through ragged mountains
On its way home.

THE HEBER CREEPER

Chugga Chug!
Chugga Chug!
Coming down the track,
I like the whistle blowing--
It scares the people back!

Laurie
Age 6

My name is Jerry
My number is seven,
In October
I'll turn eleven.

Jerry
Age 10

There was an old lady
With a wooden leg.
It was so thin
It looked like a peg.

Keith
Age 7

A CHILD'S PRESENT TO A FRIEND

I'll build my friend a mountain

Out of cars —
   Crash, bang, clickity, clack.
Out of toy clocks —
   Tick, tock, click, clock.
And out of toy frogs —
   Hop, jump, croak, croak.

My friend's mountain will sound like this:
   Crash-bang,
     tick-tock,
       Hop-jump,
         Click-clock,
           Croak-croak,
              Clickity-clack!

Alva
Age 7

EVENTIDE

The evening sky
A touch of gray
Some purple mountains
And the end of day.

The golden sun
Sets fire to the west
And then the night
Puts the sky to rest.

Jocelyn
Age 11

THE OCEAN

The lonely ocean
Cold and damp
Shivers in the frosty night.
Carrying all the boats and ships
Has made her tired.
And so she lies
In the dark night
And sleeps
Very still.

David
Age 11

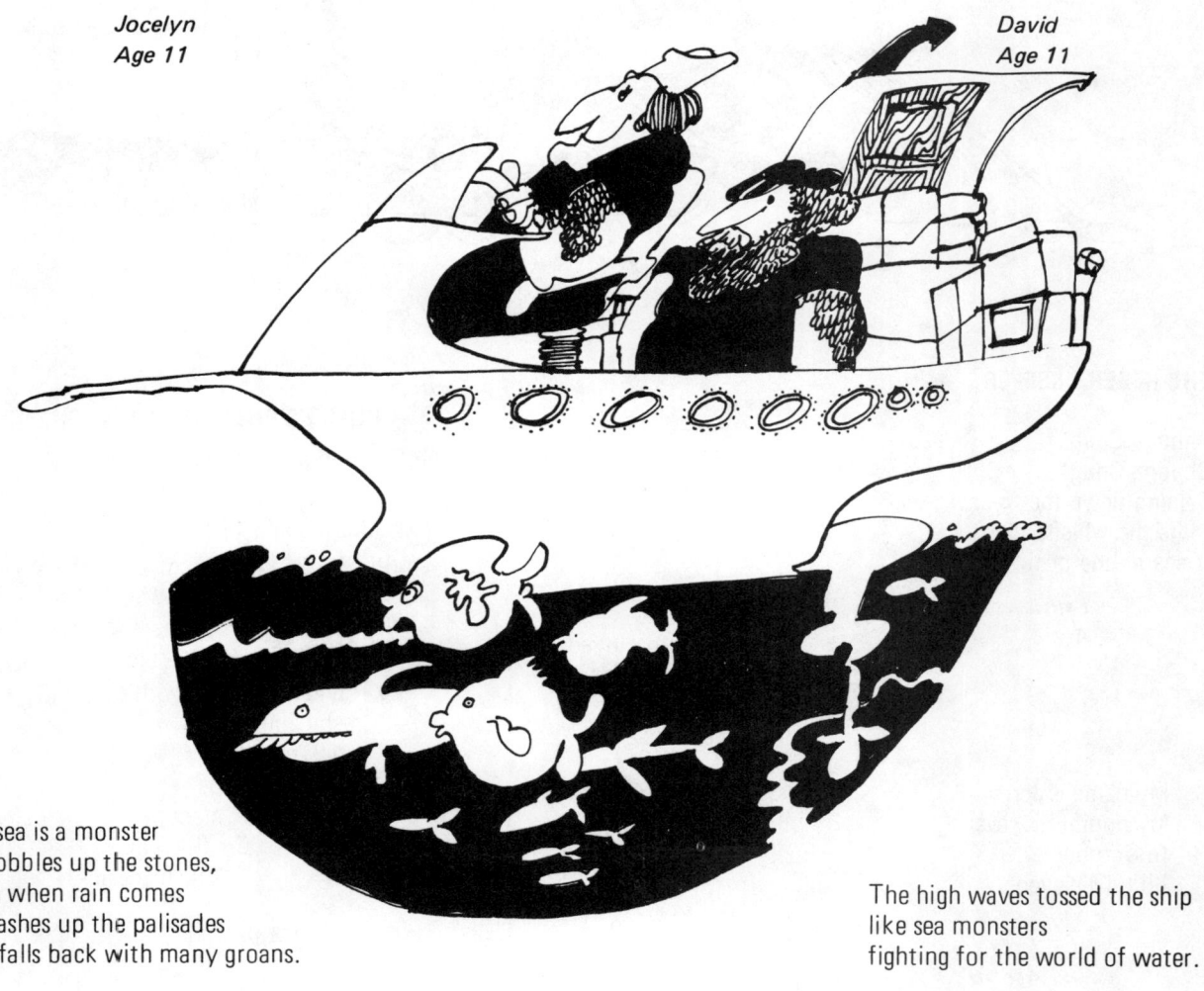

The sea is a monster
He gobbles up the stones,
Then when rain comes
He dashes up the palisades
And falls back with many groans.

Barbara
Age 9

The high waves tossed the ship
like sea monsters
fighting for the world of water.

Cindy
Age 9

ANCIENT PATTERNS

Fluorescent lamps
Glow throughout ebony trees.
The polished stream reflects the campfires.
A spider's web turns into crystal strings
    of ancient patterns.

Julie
Age 11

TALL TALE

I visited a mountain far away.
The streams were purple, the night was day.
The grass was red, the cows were green,
The pink elephants hated to be seen.
The wind blew upward, the vines grew down,
After one day —
I left for the town.

Lynne
Age 11

Raindrops fall silently
Soft mist lifts from the ground,
The storm has begun.

Sally
Age 11

There was an old lady
Who got a new shoe.
She went outside
And away she flew.

Krista
Age 7

LAGOON

The people get excited
As the roller coaster goes down the hill.
My hair flies up;
My face turns red.
The scare gives me a thrill!

Paul
Age 7

CATSUP

Catsup is a beautiful red
I love it so much it goes to my head.
I love the taste of catsup on a bun.
It certainly makes hot-dog eating fun!

Susan
Age 11

If I were an airplane pilot
I'd soar above cotton clouds
    into azure sky
And fly away to happiness!

Scott
Age 11

UNRHYMED COUPLETS

There's a mountain like a giant,
When the clouds are low, he hides.

Devin
Age 7

There's a little chick a-sleeping
Still inside a white-shelled egg.

Kristen
Age 7

See the children playing jump rope
Until the teacher calls them in.

Hear the wind go rushing by you
Making trees bend to the ground.

See the mother hen a-scratching
Finding food for baby chicks.

Watch the sun go down at sunset
See it glowing on the sea.

See the baby chicks go scratching
Looking for some little bugs.

Erin
Age 7

See the duck go gaily splashing
In a puddle rain has left.

CREDITS:
Room 10
Second Grade
Taylorsville Elementary

A car wheel sounds like
A merry-go-round
Without the music.

Sharon
Age 10

TRAVELING SOUNDS

The wheels are going fast,
And whispering very softly.
The wheels are going to sleep
Each time we ride.
Sleepy, sleepy, soft and quiet.
Sounds like singing.

Tracy
Age 10

DAN

I have a dog
His name is Dan.
He's white with spots
Of orangish-tan.

His tail is black
His nose is pink.
He swims in the bathtub
And drinks in the sink.

Dan, his eyes are red
and puffed.
Dan, my dog, he's white
and stuffed.

Sandra
Age 11

TO JONATHAN LIVINGSTON SEAGULL

Flying in the sky.
Practicing.
A very skilled seagull
Doing acrobatic stunts.
Determined to be the best,
His thoughts are on perfection.
The more he practices the better he gets.

George
Age 10

The forklift is a giant ant
Carrying loads here and there,
Running, lifting, loading.

David
Age 9

APPLES

Apples are sweet
Apples are sour
I could eat apples by the hour.
Red or green,
They are the best.
Summer or spring,
Winter or fall,
Red or green —
I eat them all.

Adrian
Age 11

DOOR TO DOOR

Avon ladies, American seeds,
Calendars and jewelry beads.
All these things go door to door.
Sell it once, then sell it some more.
Kids can do this, grown-ups, too.
All these things are just for you.
So here's some advice: Don't buy these ever.
The drug store's the best, for now and forever!

Michelle
Age 10

RHYME CUES

My teacher today showed us an old shoe.
Boy, that shoe could use lots of glue.
It could not take any more stamping.
Oh, did I tell you she found it while camping?
And now she has us writing poems.
In my poem I will name my shoe,
I think it might be Sue.
Yes, Sue is a good name for a shoe.
I think my poem will rhyme;
It shouldn't take much time,
And then it will be mine.
I will show it to my brothers
And maybe, just maybe, to others.

June
Age 11

OUR CRYSTAL GARDEN

Elegant as coral flocked flowers
Dainty drops dangling —
Dangerously sharp points.

Mike
Age 7

My name is Kasparian
   My number is seven.
      Tell me now,
         What rhymes with heaven?

Kirk
Age 11

DURING THE MIDNIGHT MOVIES...

The wind howled like a mad wolf-man
As angry as a rampaging rhinoceros.

Randy
Age 11

My name is Shayne
   My number is ten.
      I do my writing in the den!

Shayne
Age 10

Turtles snap,
Turtles fight,
   But children shouldn't
   It's not polite.

Mike
Age 7

BALLOONS

Soaring through the air
Higher and higher every minute.
Then suddenly, POP! POP!
Down they come!

Elizabeth
Age 9

RIDDLE

It has no color to its face,
And sometimes goes at a very slow pace.
There is never one like the other,
But there will always be another.

(A day)

Jan
Age 11

MY FAVORITE PLACE

Every night I like to go
    to my favorite place by the river.
It has only one tree
    but I like it.
There my giant snail greets me.
I get on his back
And hold my favorite snake
And away we go for a ride.

    Good night river
    Good night tree
    Good night snail
    And good night snake

Tomorrow night I will return
    to my favorite place!

David
Age 10

There was an old lady
Who liked to eat snacks,
Peanuts and popcorn,
Crackers and tacks.

Jacque
Age 7

My grandmother
How sweet she was.
I wish she'd have stayed —
She's long since passed away.

Mitzi
Age 11

Push along!
Through mud
    wilting weeds
        rivers dark and deep
Weary feet
    creaky wheels
Crying babies
    tired faces
Push along!

Stephanie
Age 11

This is the last
    of all my poem
Because I'm tired
    I'm going to go home!

Russell
Age 11

From My Butterfly Net

Hand-Printed Poems by Me